build your own contemporary furniture

best of popular woodworking magazine

POPULAR WOODWORKING BOOKS

CINCINNATI, OHIO
www.popularwoodworking.com

read this important safety notice

To prevent accidents, keep safety in mind while you work. Use the safety guards installed on power equipment; they are for your protection. When working on power equipment, keep fingers away from saw blades, wear safety goggles to prevent injuries from flying wood chips and sawdust, wear headphones to protect your hearing and consider installing a dust vacuum to reduce the amount of airborne sawdust in your woodshop. Don't wear loose clothing, such as neckties or shirts with loose sleeves, or jewelry, such as rings, necklaces or bracelets, when working on power equipment. Tie back long hair to prevent it from getting caught in your equipment. People who are sensitive to certain chemicals should check the chemical content of any product before using it. The authors and editors who compiled this book have tried to make the contents as accurate and correct as possible. Plans, illustrations, photographs and text have been carefully checked. All instructions, plans and projects should be carefully read, studied and understood before beginning construction. Due to the variability of local conditions, construction materials, skill levels, etc., neither the author nor Popular Woodworking Books assumes any responsibility for any accidents, injuries, damages or other losses incurred resulting from the material presented in this book. Prices listed for supplies and equipment were current at the time of publication, and are subject to change.

metric conversion chart

to convert	to	multiply by
Inches	Centimeters	2.54
Centimeters	Inches	0.4
Feet	Centimeters	30.5
Centimeters	Feet	0.03
Yards	Meters	0.9
Meters	Yards	1.1
Sq. Inches	Sq. Centimeters	6.45
Sq. Centimeters	Sq. Inches	0.16
Sq. Feet	Sq. Meters	0.09
Sq. Meters	Sq. Feet	10.8
Sq. Yards	Sq. Meters	0.8
Sq. Meters	Sq. Yards	1.2
Pounds	Kilograms	0.45
Kilograms	Pounds	2.2
Ounces	Grams	28.3
Grams	Ounces	0.035

Build Your Own Contemporary Furniture. Copyright © 2002 by Popular Woodworking Books. Manufactured in China. All rights reserved. No part of this book may be reproduced in any form or by any electronic or mechanical means including information storage and retrieval systems without permission in writing from the publisher, except by a reviewer, who may quote brief passages in a review. Published by Popular Woodworking Books, an imprint of F&W Publications, Inc., 4700 East Galbraith Road, Cincinnati, Ohio, 45236. First edition.

Visit our Web site at www.popularwoodworking.com for more information and resources for woodworkers.

Other fine Popular Woodworking Books are available from your local bookstore or direct from the publisher.

06   05   04   03   02   5   4   3   2   1

Library of Congress Cataloging-in-Publication Data
Build your own contemporary furniture: includes 20 sleek and stylish projects / by the editors of Popular Woodworking magazine.
     p. cm.
    Includes index.
    ISBN 1-55870-610-0 (alk. paper)
    1. Furniture making--Amateurs' manuals. I. Popular woodworking.

TT195 .B85 2002
684.1"04--dc21
                        2001133022

Edited by Jennifer Churchill
Content edited by Megan Williamson
Designed by Brian Roeth
Page layout by Kathy Bergstrom
Lead photography by Al Parrish
Step-by-step photography by *Popular Woodworking* staff
Production coordinated by Mark Griffin

credits

Staff of *Popular Woodworking* magazine
Christopher Schwarz, Senior Editor: Asian Coffee Table, Shoji-Paper Lamp, Step Tansu
Steve Shanesy, Editor and Publisher: Magic Shelves, Nakashima-Inspired Table, Secrets to a Silky Smooth Finish
Jim Stuard, Associate Editor: Bauhaus Jewelry Box, Contemporary Shelves, Kitchen Island, Desktop Pencil Box, Photo Screen, Dresser-top Valet
David Thiel, Senior Editor: Great Danish Modern Table, Jewelry Armoire, Modern Wardrobe, No More Miter Gauge, Sam Maloof's Sculpted-Base Table
David Thiel, Senior Editor, and **Gregory Crofton:** Guest Room Murphy Bed

contributors

Mark Kessler: Modern Console, Side Table
Troy Sexton: Closet Overhaul, Compact Entertainment Unit

Modern Console: ©2002 by Mark Kessler. All rights reserved. Originally appeared in April 2000 *Popular Woodworking* magazine.
Side Table: © 2002 by Mark Kessler. All rights reserved. Originally appeared in November 1999 *Popular Woodworking* magazine.
Closet Overhaul: © 2002 by Troy Sexton. All rights reserved. Originally appeared in January 2000 *Popular Woodworking* magazine.
Compact Entertainment Unit: © 2002 by Troy Sexton. All rights reserved. Originally appeared in November 1999 *Popular Woodworking* magazine.

INTRODUCTION

The word contemporary, when used to describe a style of furniture, is somewhat ambiguous. By definition, contemporary means marked by characteristics of the present time period, but in the woodworking world, it has come to describe furniture that doesn't fit into any particular style of the past 60 to 70 years. Contemporary generally means furniture from the 1950s to the present.

Contemporary furniture usually has clean, straight and/or curved design lines, very little ornamentation in the form of carving, profiling or appliqués. Exotic wood veneers are used to decorate the furniture. Flat doors and drawer fronts are common, as are plain-paneled cabinet sides.

In the late 1970s, the use of solid wood to build furniture came back into common practice. Locally grown wood that was suitable for building furniture was used by furniture makers because it was easier to find and purchase. This use of inexpensive, locally grown wood is still common today in the building of contemporary furniture, with exotic hardwoods from the rain forests of the world used as accents.

Joinery used to assemble contemporary furniture is indicative of the times. Today, biscuit joinery, knockdown joinery and screws are used profusely in furniture making. If traditional joinery (e.g., dovetail, mortise and tenon or bridle) is used, it is often exposed in order to give the furniture a look of strength and elegance, while at the same time showing off the builder's skill. Also, the woods used are carefully chosen for their unusual color and markings.

In this day and time, the variety of furniture-making materials available to the home woodworker is amazing. Everything from metal drawer slides to any style of hinges, pulls or knobs are available at local hardware and woodworking centers. In most large metropolitan areas, any type of wood is available in any form (i.e., plywood, particleboard, medium-density fiberboard, exotic hardwoods, domestic hardwoods or single sheets of veneer).

We encourage you, the home woodworker, to buy your materials carefully and to remain mindful of the wasteful nature of some manufacturing processes. Buy from local businesses as much as possible and carefully plan your projects so that material waste is kept to a minimum.

The contemporary projects in this book utilize a range of materials and techniques, so there is something for every woodworker out there. We hope you enjoy building these projects and that they will find a place in your home.

Now, on with the projects and have fun!

TABLE OF CONTENTS

TECHNIQUES

The projects in this book range from basic to intermediate in terms of the woodworking skills needed to build them.

We wanted to help you, the reader, to have an enjoyable time building these projects, so we've included a very easy to build, yet very precise, combination table saw sled and miter guage. This tool will enable you to cut very accurate, clean and crisp miters everytime. Repeated cuts are as easy as setting the stop block on the sled's fence. The fence can be set in a matter of seconds to cut miters (and the stop block will work on this fence too).

Also included with the table saw sled is a hold-down and a featherboard so you can work in safety. All the hardware needed to make this awesome sled is readily available at any hardware store or home-improvment center.

The other great technique included here is how to get that smooth-as-glass finish everytime. Finishing your prize project is not as scary as you might think. Just like building a project one step at a time, we show you how to get that finish you've always dreamed of— one step at a time.

Wheather you spray, brush or wipe-on your finish, you can enhance that final sheen and feel by learning how to "rub it out" (polish it) with a minimum amount of hassle. No need to worry that you're going to ruin the finish you just applied. Rest assured that you will become the master-finisher you were meant to be!

NO MORE miter gauge

I'VE TRIED OUT DOZENS OF table saws over the years, and the one thing I've come to expect on all makes and models is the miter gauge that barely serves its purpose. Catalogs have come to the rescue with many excellent after-market miter gauge replacements — but what a price! I figured I'm reasonably intelligent, so I should be able to make my own replacement for a lot less. Voilá, for less than $35 in hardware and a modest amount of wood, I'm set. You can do it too — just follow the steps.

Split Rail Fencing

I took the improved miter gauge concept a step further and turned it into a miter sled. This gives me the opportunity to add a stop block with measuring tape, as well as a hold-down attachment. The sled itself is simply a piece of ½" Baltic birch plywood attached to the guide bar from my old miter gauge. The part that makes this table saw jig versatile happens at the fence.

Both the permanent fence and the miter fence are made the same way on the table saw. Start with four "halves" and mark the inside face and top surface. Next, set up the saw as shown in the photos and make mirror-image grooves the length of the fence parts.

To allow for some adjustability on the fixed fence, use a chisel to carefully cut matching notches on both fence halves. When the halves are glued together, the notches will allow a screw head to slide ½" to allow you to square up your fence to the saw blade.

When done making those cuts, check the slots' fit against the hardware, then glue the halves together using the top surface, rather than the bottom, as the reference point. When the glue has cured, run the bottom edge of each fence over the jointer to make a square and even bottom surface. Then reset the jointer fence to a 45° angle and take a pass (or two) off the

You don't have to spend $200 to make dead-on crosscuts and miters; we built this sled for $35 in hardware.

Make miter cuts with this sure-grip hold-down

Use the attachable featherboard for repeat cuts.

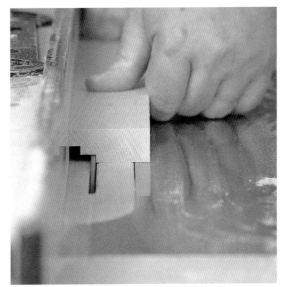

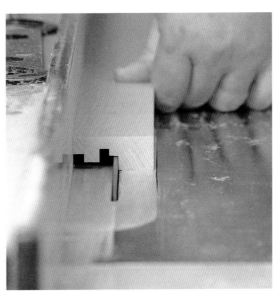

inside bottom edge of each fence to make a dust slot. This slot keeps any chips or dirt from holding your work away from the fence.

Mending Fences

The next step is to prepare the fences for attachment to the sled. This is where the fences become different. The fixed fence is attached with machine screws slipped through clearance holes in the fence and fastened to T-nuts recessed into the underside of the sled. Location of the clearance holes isn't critical, but the fence should be clamped in place (flush to the right edge of the sled) before drilling the holes. Start by cutting the fences to length.

The hole necessary for the barrel of the T-nut is larger in diameter than the clearance hole for the screw, so you can drill a clearance hole straight through the fence

and through the sled. The fixed screw hole at the right of the fence should then be counterbored to allow the screw's head to drop below the groove. The machine screw's head should be no larger than ³/₈" to clear the fence grooves.

The adjustable screw (on the left of the fence) has already been notched in the previous step, so all that's left is to drill the T-nut holes to the proper diameter and recess the holes ¹/₈" from the underside using a Forstner bit.

The miter fence is a little easier. Angle-cut the ends of the fence to form a tongue on each end and then round them. The ¹/₄" clearance holes are drilled in the center and ³/₄" in from the ends. The T-nuts are then inserted as before with locations on the sled for 15°, 22.5°, 30° and 45° stops.

Adjustable Stop

The stop attachment is designed to be used on either the fixed or mitering fence. Shown in a detailed diagram on the following page, the stop is simply four pieces of wood and a clear plastic insert. The stop's top is first grooved and notched for the Plexiglas window, then two slots are formed by connecting drilled holes to allow the Plexiglas to be adjusted on the measuring tape as necessary.

Glue the face plate to the underside of the top and glue a guide to the underside of the top to fit into the groove in the fences. Some fine adjustment may be necessary to allow the stop attachment to move freely. Use the stop arm in the diagrams to cut and shape the arm. Then lightly clamp the arm in place, drill a clearance hole and screw the arm to the stop. With the arm in place, use a scratch awl to

cutting list (inches): *miter sled*

No.	Ltr.	Item	Dimensions T W L	Material
1	A	Sled	$1/2$" x 20" x 24"	Plywood
4	B	Fence halves	$3/4$" x 2" x 24"	Maple
1	C	Stop top	$1/2$" x $2^{1}/_{8}$" x 4"	Plywood
1	D	Stop face	$1/2$" x $1^{7}/_{8}$" x 4"	Plywood
1	E	Stop arm	$1/2$" x $2^{1}/_{4}$" x $2^{1}/_{4}$"	Plywood
2	F	Stop guides	$3/16$" x $3/4$" x 4"	Maple
1	G	Stop window	$3/16$" x $3/8$" x $4^{7}/_{8}$"	Plexiglas
1	H	Hold-down top	$3/4$" x $1^{9}/_{16}$" x 4"	Maple
1	I	Hold-down face	$1/2$" x $5^{1}/_{4}$" x $3^{1}/_{2}$"	Plywood

HARDWARE:

2 - $5/16$" x 18 x $3^{1}/_{2}$" T-slot bolts*   2 - $5/16$" - 18 knobs*
1 - $5/16$" x 18 x $1^{1}/_{2}$" furniture glide*   7 - $1/4$" - 20 T-nuts*
1 - 24" right-to-left read tape**   1 - $3/8$" - 16 T-nut*
2 - $1/4$" x 20 x $1^{1}/_{4}$" stemmed knobs   6 - $1/4$" washers
2 - $1/4$" x 20 threaded inserts*   2 - $1/4$" - 20 x 1" knobs
2 - #6 x $3/8$" roundhead screws
1 - #6 x 1" roundhead screw

*Available from Rockler, www.rockler.com (800) 279-4441
**Available from Woodhaven, www.woodhaven.com (800) 344-6657

cutting list (millimeters): *miter sled*

No.	Ltr.	Item	Dimensions T W L	Material
1	A	Sled	13 x 508 x 610	Plywood
4	B	Fence halves	19 x 51 x 610	Maple
1	C	Stop top	13 x 54 x 102	Plywood
1	D	Stop face	13 x 47 x 102	Plywood
1	E	Stop arm	13 x 57 x 57	Plywood
2	F	Stop guides	21 x 19 x 102	Maple
1	G	Stop window	21 x 10 x 124	Plexiglas
1	H	Hold-down top	19 x 39 x 102	Maple
1	I	Hold-down face	13 x 133 x 89	Plywood

HARDWARE:

2 - 8mm - 18 x $3^{1}/_{2}$" T-slot bolts*   2 - 8mm - 18 knobs*
1 - 8mm - 18 x $1^{1}/_{2}$" furniture glide*   7 - 6mm - 20 T-nuts*
1 - 610mm right-to-left read tape**   1 - 10mm - 16 T-nut*
2 - 6mm - 20 x $1^{1}/_{4}$"stemmed knobs   6 - 6mm washers
2 - 6mm - 20 threaded inserts*   2 - 6mm - 20 x 1" knobs
2 - #6 x 10mm roundhead screws
1 - #6 x 25mm roundhead screw

*Available from Rockler, www.rockler.com (800) 279-4441
**Available from Woodhaven, www.woodhaven.com (800) 344-6657

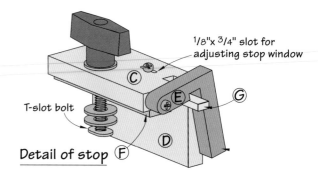

$1/8$"x $3/4$" slot for adjusting stop window

T-slot bolt

Detail of stop Ⓕ

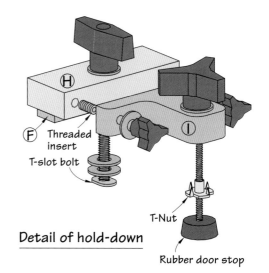

Detail of hold-down

Threaded insert

T-slot bolt

T-Nut

Rubber door stop

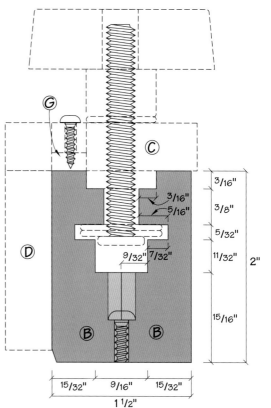

$3/16$"
$3/8$"
$5/32$"
$11/32$"
$15/16$"
2"
$3/16$"
$5/16$"
$9/32$" $7/32$"

$15/32$" $9/16$" $15/32$"
$1^{1}/_{2}$"

Full-size profile

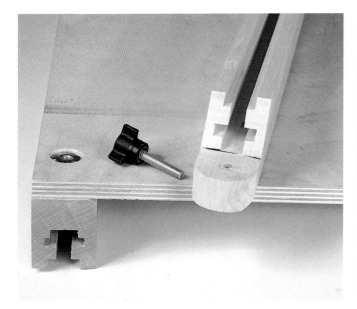

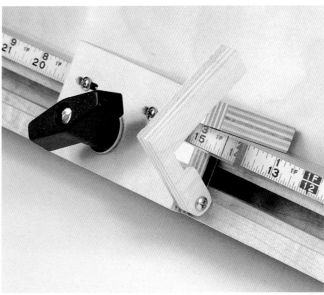

2 Threaded inserts could be used to attach the fences to the sled, but they always seem to go in crooked. T-nuts are cheaper, easier to install and provide positive pull from the underside flange. One end of each fence and the recessed T-nuts are shown in the photo above. The last step on the fixed fence is to attach the right-to-left-reading adhesive measuring tape.

3 A feature we enjoy on this stop is the swing-up stop arm. This allows you to square cut one end of your piece (arm up), then swing the arm down and make the final length cut. No resetting necessary. The hash mark on the window is set to the final cut size.

4 By using optional add-ons for the hold-down attachment, this hold-down serves two functions. You might think of a few more add-ons to make the miter sled even more versatile.

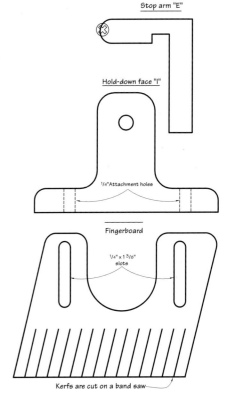

Stop arm "E"

Hold-down face "I"

¼" Attachment holes

Fingerboard

¼" x 1 ³⁄₈" slots

Kerfs are cut on a band saw

Enlarge 200% for full-size diagrams.

cut a groove in the Plexiglas, then use a dark putty stick to fill in the groove. Wipe away the excess.

Hold-Down

Sometimes a stop block isn't what you want. What you need is a hold-down device. To provide the most versatility, I opted for a convertible hold-down attachment. Using a top assembly similar to the stop attachment, I mounted two threaded inserts into the facing edge of the top and made two different hold-down attachments for different applications. The feather-

board adjusts up and down to hold the work in place for repeat passes such as dadoes, while allowing enough play to tap the piece over for the next pass. A rubber door-stop on a piece of threaded rod with a handle locks the piece in place and keeps it there. Again, the handy T-nut comes into play.

I'm fairly certain some of our readers will take the ideas presented here and make them even better. And even if you don't make any changes I guarantee you'll find this sled more useful than your "factory" miter slot gauge. ■

secrets TO A SILKY SMOOTH FINISH

Ignore the oddballs who spend hours massaging a finish. Here's how to do the job quickly and easily.

LEARNING TO COMPLETE YOUR finish, more often called "rubbing out," will do more to improve the quality of your woodworking than anything else, period. (OK, that assumes you already know how to glue parts together so they don't come apart.) It's the secret to a silky, satiny, even mirror-like finish, and it will take away all your stress about dust, lint, hair, even assorted bugs settling into that wet coat you just carefully applied. In fact, you won't even have to worry so much about applying your finish quite so carefully.

Best of all, it's sooo easy.

Basically, I'm talking about rubbing out your finish. But first I want to assure you that I won't ask you to spend hours massaging your project with #0000 steel wool. And I'm not going to ask you to buy pumice, or rottenstone, or rubbing and polishing compounds. You'll only need those products if you're going for the ultimate high-polish mirror finish, which I do with about the same regularity as a visit from Halley's Comet!

No, all I want you to do is hand sand your finish (not the bare wood, but the varnish, shellac, lacquer or polyurethane), with two or three different grit sandpapers. It's so simple, you won't want to tell anyone how you did it because the fantastic results look like it ought to require a lot more work.

Which Finishes Rub Out Best

The method I'll describe here will work on any common film-forming finish. It is easiest and will produce the best results on

Don't try this at home. To prove just how effective wetsanding is at giving your project a glass-like sheen, we sprinkled a handful of sawdust on some wet shellac. After rubbing it out, no one in the office could tell that the finish had ever been boogered up. See the sidebar "Goobers Begone!" to see how we did this.

lacquer and shellac, but you'll still get incredible results with varnish (including polyurethane varnish) and water-based finishes.

Shellac and lacquer work best because the dried film, although hard, still is softer than water-based finishes and varnish (which is sold almost always as polyurethane). This property makes it sand faster, so it's easier. Also, the scratches from the sanding are smoother, producing a clearer sheen. But in no way let this discourage you from applying these techniques to your varnish and water-based finishes.

Sanding the First Coat

You complete your finish after your first coat or sealer coat has been applied and has had time to dry. Drying time will vary greatly depending on the finish you're using. Basically, it's dry enough when it doesn't "ball up" on the sandpaper. For this first sanding, use what's called a "self-lubricating" aluminum oxide sandpaper. It is self lubricating because it has a special powder that helps prevent sanding dust from sticking in the abrasive grit and clogging it up. One common brand of such sandpaper is 3M Tri-M-ite.

To sand, use moderate pressure to sand off the fuzzy-feeling "nibs," or all the little imperfections that make the first coat rough to the touch. In smoothing this first coat, you are preparing a surface for the application of the next coat. The objective is to begin producing an ideal surface. Think of glass as a perfect surface. If you brushed or sprayed a finish on it, it would lay out and form a perfectly smooth film.

In addition to sanding off the nibs, you also want to begin "leveling" your first coat of finish. This will include high spots from lapping brush strokes, or runs or sags on vertical surfaces. If you finish open-grained woods such as oak, ash, walnut or mahogany, leveling also will begin knocking down the "peaks" of finish created by the "valleys" of the open grain.

A word of caution is in order, particularly if you are working with a project that has any type of color applied, such as a stain or dye. If you sand too much, you will sand, or "cut," through the film and likely sand away the applied color. Edges are especially vulnerable and require a deli-

Goobers Begone!

To fix the goober, first let the finish dry completely and don't be tempted to try to fish out that errant hair, fly or dust speck. You'll only create a bigger problem. Next, lightly sand the finish in the dust-strewn area with 220-grit paper, dry. Try to get the surface as level as possible to the surrounding finish. Next, apply another coat of finish and let it dry completely. Proceed with wet-sanding and presto, you'll wonder where the sawdust went.

A close-up of the accumulated dust to show just how bad a problem it is.

Much better than new. The massive sawdust defect is virtually eliminated. Need you ever worry about finishing in a "dust free" area again?

Here's a close-up of what the finish looks like after a first coat of lacquer on walnut, which is an open-grained wood. The finish will feel fuzzy and the grain will look hilly. The object is to remove these fuzzy nibs and level the finish so the next coat of finish will lay flat.

Sanding the first, or sealer coat, with 360-grit dry-lube sandpaper is the first step in rubbing out, or completing, your finish. This sanding is the first step in preparing the surface for the next coat of finish and begins leveling the surface. Use a full sheet of sandpaper folded twice under the flat of your hand (inset). Then add another coat of finish. At this stage, your finish will begin leveling, seriously reducing the open-grain look of a non-sanded finish.

Wetsanding will open new worlds of better finishes for you. Use 400-grit wet/dry sandpaper and a lubricating liquid such as paint thinner or soapy water to allow the fine abrasive to work without becoming clogged (see inset).

A final wetsanding with 600-grit wet/dry sandpaper will produce a higher sheen if desired. This sanding should go quickly because the objective is only to eliminate the coarser sanding scratches from the previous sanding, not leveling the surface further.

If you choose, you can take your finish to an even higher level of sheen by rubbing it out with polishing compounds and very fine steel wool. However, I recommend this only for your most important projects.

If you do decide to use steel wool in the final polishing of your project, here's the right way to use it. Unfold the pad completely and then fold it over on itself once. Then use the flat of your hand to press the steel wool against the wood.

cate touch.

Now that you have completed your first level of surface preparation, dust off the work and apply more finish material. If you are brushing with a varnish, polyurethane or water base, one coat is probably enough. If you are brushing or spraying shellac or lacquer, apply at least three coats. Again, allow sufficient drying time between coats and before the next sanding step.

Wetsanding: A Brave New World

If wetsanding is new to you, you'll be amazed at how efficient it is when applied to your finish. For sandpaper, switch to 400-grit wet/dry sandpaper. This is a paper with a special adhesive that won't dissolve in the liquid, and the paper itself will hold up as well.

Wetsanding works because the liquid you use both lubricates between the surface and the sandpaper and flushes away the material that is being removed by the sanding process.

When wetsanding, I like to use a half sheet of sandpaper that has been folded twice. Some finishers prefer to wetsand with a block that has a piece of $\frac{1}{4}$" cork glued on the sole. Using a block can help make sure you sand flat continually and

some might argue it helps prevent cutting through the finish, but it can give the user a false sense of security.

The liquid I prefer for wetsanding is paint thinner. You can also use water that's had a few drops of liquid dish detergent added. Paint thinner works best because it's more efficient at flushing away the sanded finish residue. We all know that water on wood and wood finishes has some inherent problems, especially if the end grain isn't completely sealed.

So is wetsanding a tedious, time-consuming chore? Clearly, it adds a couple more steps to the finish process, but if your goal is simply a nice, slicked-up finish, it really doesn't take all that much extra work. For example, the walnut sample board in the photos is about 18" × 36" and it took me no more than 10 to 12 minutes to wetsand it each time. In some respects, it may save you some time. If you've been led to believe the nutballs who insist you finish in a "dust free" environment, forget it. Let me save you some time because it may take you less time to wetsand than create a "clean" room. You'll also benefit from not being concerned about goobers falling in your not-quite-dry finish.

Now, depending on the type of finish

and sheen you want, you can proceed with another round of applying clear finish and wetsanding a last time, or you can basically call your finish done, except for a final coat of wax. Of course, before you complete the job with a coat of wax, clean all the messy sanding slurry off the work. For this chore, use either paint thinner or VMP naphtha on a clean rag.

On tight-grained woods such as cherry, maple, birch or a softwood such as pine, you will have a smooth, flat, closed-pore finish with a medium sheen. With open-grained woods such as walnut or mahogany, the finish will be either an open or semi-open pore finish. The distinction is simply a matter of the degree of wood grain that's not filled up and leveled off.

To achieve a fully filled finish on open-grained wood that's not been grain-filled, you'll need to proceed with another coat of finish and another wetsanding. Follow the procedure as before. By the end of this stage your finish should be done except for a coat of wax.

Should you want a higher level of sheen, wetsand one last time using 600-grit wet/dry sandpaper.

It would be at this stage that you would continue working with various levels of rubbing and polishing compounds if you wanted to create a high-polish finish. Frankly, it would take a pretty special project for me to go to that level of a finish.

In fact, I'd even make a strong recommendation that when you decide to wetsand a project, you might even skip certain parts of the project altogether. For example, it would be good to wetsand a tabletop but not the legs. Or the top of a desk but not the sides. In other words, only the most prominent and visible features. Generally speaking, it would be very difficult to wetsand the details on turned or carved work.

If you forgo wetsanding part of a project, it may, however, be necessary to rub out the entire piece with #0000 steel wool or a synthetic steel wool product like 3M's Scotch Brite pads. This will impart a consistent level of sheen to the entire project.

You should also consider using only gloss finish on projects you intend to wetsand. Not only will the gloss finish material make the finish look clearer, but the final sheen will be derived from the wetsanding or rubbing. ∎

nakashima-inspired
TABLE

The first furniture to come from harvesting a backyard cherry tree pays tribute to master woodworker, furniture designer and national treasure, George Nakashima.

MOST OF THE LUMBER USED BY GEORGE Nakashima was sawn from the log under his supervision, stacked in the order in which it was cut, then stickered and left to air dry before kiln drying. At his disposal were thousands of boards which were sawn "through and through," retaining each board's waney or "free" edge and unique shape. And because the logs were not sawn for grade, when the log is turned time and again during the sawing to avoid defects such as knots and splits, these "flaws" were retained and often became an important feature in the use of the board.

NEEDLESS TO SAY, MOST WOOD-workers don't have easy access to wood that has been processed this way. But I had the opportunity when a black cherry in my backyard fell prey to a hard, late frost and succumbed. Within a few weeks I engaged the operator of a Wood-Mizer portable band saw mill and had the log sawn where it fell. The going rate for this work is about 45 cents a board foot. About 18 months later, having stacked it carefully for air drying, I was ready to start working it. Now, if you don't have access to lumber like this, you could always make a rectangular top.

From my boards I selected a shorter one that came from the top of the log where the tree began to branch. This area is referred to as a "crotch" and usually yields nicely figured material. But this part of the tree also has a lot of stress in the lumber and often wants to split during drying. True to form, a wide check occurred on the end.

Never mind, I decided, I'll work with it. The grain is just too pretty to toss in the scrap box.

The 17"-wide board was also cupped starting at the heart's center. To flatten the board, even if I had a jointer or planer that wide, would have sacrificed too much thickness. However, sawing lengthwise along the heart, splitting the board in two, rendered two relatively flat pieces. It was at this point I decided to the use an open spline detail of contrasting walnut to join the pieces back together. The decision made the technical necessity of splitting the boards an interesting design element.

After the top was separated, I smoothed and flattened the pieces using a Performax 22"-wide belt sander. When done, I routed a $\frac{1}{2}$" × $\frac{5}{8}$"-deep groove in the edges to be joined, and then I cut a walnut spline that was $1\frac{7}{16}$" wide. That left a $\frac{3}{16}$" gap when the top was glued back together. Before

The Extraordinary Life of Nakashima

Among woodworkers, none has expressed through design and use an unabashed reverence for wood as a material like George Nakashima. He strongly believed the objects he designed and built were giving a once-living tree a second life, and it was his objective to allow the natural beauty of the wood he was working to showcase itself.

His design skills in furniture were absolutely unique, forging cross-cultural and cross-generational lines. You see in his furniture the western influence of modernism, Arts & Crafts and Shaker styles wonderfully blended with the simple yet powerful Japanese design, expression of materials and the exacting execution of woodworking skills.

He was born in Spokane, Washington, in 1905, and was awarded a master's degree in Architecture from the Massachusetts Institute of Technology (MIT). Later he traveled by steamer to Paris and to Japan, where he lived for a number of years. While there he became immersed in his Japanese heritage and worked in the Tokyo office of an architectural firm owned by a Czech- American. He was sent to India by the firm to supervise the construction of a building at an ashram. He returned to Japan briefly before returning home in 1940. Two years later, he and his family were interned with most Japanese-Americans living on the West coast as the United States went to war with Japan. At the Idaho internment camp he learned traditional Japanese woodworking methods from an older resident.

After his release from the camp, Nakashima moved to eastern Pennsylvania where he established a home, a shop and a design studio. Over the years his furniture was collected by numerous wealthy clients. His work has been exhibited at most major art museums. In 1952 he was awarded the Gold Medal of Craftsmanship by the American Institute of Architects, and in 1979 he was named a fellow by the American Crafts Council. In 1989 the American Crafts Museum in New York selected his work as the first exhibit in a series called "America's Living National Treasures." The following year, Nakashima died. His workshop and studio continue to operate today under the direction of his Harvard-educated daughter, Mira Nakashima-Yarnall. The expression of his work, design and philosophical approach to both is wonderfully captured in his book *The Soul of a Tree* (Kodansha International Ltd.). In it he wrote, "Each plank...can have only one ideal use. The woodworker must find this ideal use and create an object of utility to man, and if nature smiles, an object of lasting beauty."

1 In the center of the bottom edge of the panel end, use a trim piece of the actual beam to mark the outline of the dovetail that is to be cut. With the dovetail shape already cut on the beam, an accurate layout is assured.

2 Cut the dovetail sides using a saw without a back (because the cut is nearly 3" deep). Be sure when you start the cut that the saw is properly aligned on both faces of the panel. Make the cut slowly until you've established the saw kerf following the layout line.

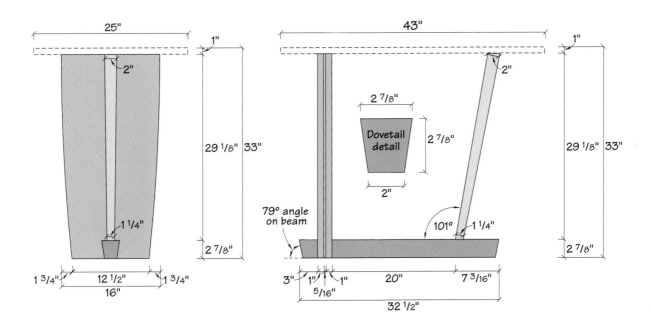

cutting list (inches): *nakashima-inspired table*

No.	Item	Dimensions T W L
1	Top	1" x 25" x 43"
2	Panel ends	1" x 16" x 32"
2	Panel buildups	$5/16$" x 3" x 32"
1	Panel buildup	$5/16$" x 5" x 32"
1	Leg	2" x 2" x 31"
1	Beam	$2^7/8$" x $2^7/8$" x $32^1/2$"

cutting list (millimeters): *nakashima-inspired table*

No.	Item	Dimensions T W L
1	Top	25 x 635 x 1092
2	Panel ends	25 x 406 x 813
2	Panel buildups	8 x 76 x 813
1	Panel buildup	8 x 127 x 813
1	Leg	51 x 51 x 787
1	Beam	73 x 73 x 826

3 After sawing out the bulk of the waste with a coping saw, chisel the remaining waste. Make certain your cuts are perpendicular to the face. After cutting halfway down, turn the panel over and work from the other side to avoid tear-out.

4 Each edge of the leg panel has a slight bevel detail that's made with a hand plane or a spokeshave.

5 The tapered leg is joined to the bottom beam with two $1/2$" dowels. Although the spacing is tight, two dowels can be used. Use a doweling jig for alignment, and depending on placement, make sure you don't drill too deep.

gluing I used a block plane to make a slight chamfer on the top edges of the open joint.

Working the Free Edges

Needless to say, the bark had to be removed from the edges of the board down to the sapwood. With dry wood, the bark pops off quite easily. You can use just about any tool from a chisel to a screwdriver to knock or pry the bark off. Just be sure you don't gouge the surface you want to eventually display. To further prepare the rear edge of the top, sand it by hand with 120-grit paper. On what I considered the front edge, I used a gouge to make small facets in the surface, giving the edge a more interesting visual and tactile surface. Afterward I sanded the edge lightly.

I moved on to the area of the big check on the board's end. The inside surfaces of the crack were rough and needed smoothing. While I didn't want to make the edges look like a polished surface, neither did I want the torn fibers and rough surfaces. My solution was to use 100-grit C-weight sandpaper to get into the crack any way possible. At this point, except for final sanding of the top and ends, the hardest part of the job was completed.

The Base

The base is absolutely simple to construct, even easier than a conventional table with legs and aprons. A slab end, a dovetail-shaped beam and a tapered, angled leg is all there is to it.

To make the slab end, I started with two panels that were about an inch thick each. My plan was to glue them together as a sandwich with a $5/16$"-thick buildup in the center that, when set back from the edge, created a reveal that mimicked the spline detail on the table top.

To do this, I first made a template of the gently curved convex taper for the slab edges. I then penciled the shape onto the individual pieces and cut the shapes on the band saw. Next I used the panel's edge to transfer the shape to the buildup pieces to make the reveal. These were band sawn and the face edge cleaned up with a hand plane. I cut one additional piece of buildup to use in the center of the panel so that when cutting the through dovetail for the beam I'd have solid wood throughout.

Next I glued the panels by first gluing

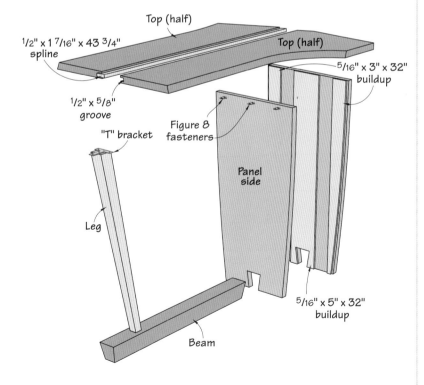

Top (half)

$1/2$" x 1 $7/16$" x 43 $3/4$" spline

Top (half)

$5/16$" x 3" x 32" buildup

$1/2$" x $5/8$" groove

Figure 8 fasteners

"T" bracket

Panel side

Leg

$5/16$" x 5" x 32" buildup

Beam

6 Transfer the dowel hole locations using dowel centers. A slight tap on the top of the legs drives the center point of the dowel center into the beam. Then drill the holes.

and nailing the buildup to one piece, maintaining a $5/16$" setback at the edges, then gluing the second panel to it. I was careful not to apply too much glue to prevent a lot of squeeze-out in the reveal.

While the glue was drying, I started making the hefty beam that ties the panel and leg together. I didn't have any stock thick enough to make the 3" × 3" blank size, so I glued three pieces of 1" stock together. After the glue dried, I cleaned and squared two opposing edges on the jointer, then planed the remaining two. Next, I sawed the blank to the dovetail shape, sloping the sides to an 8° angle. At this point I sliced off a small piece of one end that served as a template for marking the cut to be made in the bottom edge of the panel.

After marking the centers of the template and panel bottom edge, I cut the sloping slides of the dovetail using the ripping teeth of my Japanese pull saw. Next I removed most of the waste with a coping saw then chiseled the edge flat. I found the fit of the beam just a bit tight so I pared the sides of the panel dovetail opening until achieving a fit that went together with just a slight amount of force. I then removed the beam

and made the 11° bevel cuts on the ends. To complete the work on the panel I put a slight bevel on the panel edges. A hand plane was the tool of choice for this chore.

The leg that supports the other end of the table is simple enough to make. I started with a blank that was 2" square. I wanted the leg to taper from top to bottom so I penciled lines to follow on the band saw. After cutting, I cleaned the edges with the jointer.

The leg cants at a 101° angle so I chopped the bottom edge at 11°. To determine the length, I simply set the leg on the beam with the bottom edge seated evenly and the side touching the top edge of the panel. I made the mark there and made the final 11° cut on the top of the leg.

The leg is joined to the beam using two $1/2$" dowels. First drill dowel holes into the bottom of the leg; then, after inserting dowel centers, mark the dowel locations in the beam. It is then a simple task to drill the holes.

To assemble the base I used polyurethane glue because of its superior bonding characteristics in gluing non-long-grain to long-grain joints. I first glued the beam to the panel making sure the beam and panel were square. After this dried, I finished gluing the leg to the beam using a band clamp with a little assistance from a

pipe clamp to maintain the desired angle.

Fastening the top to the base was a snap. On the top edge of the panel end I used three figure-eight fasteners, setting them flush. For the leg, I used a common T-shaped bracket that I screwed onto the leg, then to the top.

To finish, I sanded everything to 150 grit and broke all the sharp edges. Next I mixed small but equal amounts of Olympic-brand Early American and Red Oak oil stain and combined seven teaspoons of this blend with a pint of boiled linseed oil. The diluted color won't blotch the cherry but will give the wood a nice color to start. Time will enrich the color more, encouraged by the linseed oil, which speeds the photochemical reaction that occurs naturally in cherry. After wiping away all excess oil, I let the prefinish dry for two days. I completed the finish with a clear top coat of lacquer, although any clear coat will work fine.

I was quite pleased with the outcome of the table. Realizing this style may not be everyone's cup of tea, I think most woodworkers would have to agree on one thing: Using the free edge of boards sawn straight off the log and showcasing "defects" in the lumber clearly celebrates the material we all enjoy using so much. It instantly reminds us of just where all the wonderful wood we use comes from. ∎

asian COFFEE TABLE

A simple design that stores a surprisingly large number of books and magazines.

MOST COFFEE TABLES ARE ILL-EQUIPPED TO handle the stresses of modern-day life. Company is coming, and your living room is strewn with books, woodworking catalogs and your spouse's magazines. Most coffee tables offer only a puny shelf to help you tidy up in a hurry. This coffee table does double duty by giving you a shelf for books and two drawers big enough to handle all but the largest publications. And oh yes, you can serve coffee on it, too.

CONSTRUCTION IS SIMPLE BUT sturdy. You build the bottom case that holds the drawers out of plywood and biscuits. Then you screw the solid maple legs onto the case and cover all the plywood edges with moulding and veneer tape. Finally, you screw the top to the legs using figure-eight fasteners and build some quick drawers. And this project won't cost you a heck of a lot, either. You need about one-third of a sheet of maple plywood (birch will do just fine, too), about four board feet of 8/4 maple and about 10 board feet of 5/4 maple. You'll also need a little Baltic birch ply and a small amount of ¼" ply for the drawer bottoms.

Start at the Top

When you're at the lumberyard, be sure to pick through the racks of soft maple for this project. Soft maple (Acer rubrum) is a little cheaper than hard maple (Acer saccharum) and is more likely to have some curl or other figure. After you plane your maple down to 1" thickness, get ready to glue up your top. I like to cut a few biscuit slots in the mating edges of the top pieces. This doesn't add to the strength of this long-grain joint, but it sure helps keep your boards in line when gluing up your panels. Clamp up your top and set it aside for the glue to dry.

Building the Lower Case

The case that holds the drawers goes together really fast. Cut out the parts you need according to the cutting list. Then cut the biscuit slots to attach the sides, back and divider between the top and bottom pieces. Take some care when locating the center divider to save yourself a headache when making the drawers. See the photo on this page for the trick to cutting biscuit slots in the middle of a panel.

Now put glue and biscuits in all the biscuit slots and clamp up the lower case. When the glue is dry, sand the case to 150 grit and turn your attention to the legs. To make attaching the legs to the case easier, go ahead and cut some clearance holes in the case's sides where the case will be joined to the back legs. This is easier to do from the outside before the legs go on.

1 Biscuiting plywood into the middle of a panel can be a layout nightmare. Or it can be a breeze. Here's the breeze way: Find the exact center of the panel and mark a line that's a hair shy of ³/₈" off from that (plywood isn't ³/₄" thick). Place the divider in place on the panel, lying flat as shown in the photo. Clamp it in place and mark the divider for a couple biscuits. Retract or remove the fence from your biscuit joiner. Cut the slots in the divider with the biscuit joiner flat on the panel. Then turn your tool around as shown in the photo and cut the slots in the panel. Use the same marks on the divider to position your tool.

Attach the Legs

Here's how to attach the legs: Mark on the leg where the case should meet the leg. Clamp the leg into place on the lower case and then drill pilot holes and clearance holes for No. 8 screws (I used a bit that drills both holes simultaneously). The holes should go through the case sides and into the legs. After the holes are drilled, screw the legs in place. Do three legs this way and clamp up the fourth leg but don't drill your holes yet.

You want to make sure that your table sits perfectly level — especially if you have hardwood floors. Place the table on a surface that you know is flat: your bench or a couple sheets of plywood. Then see if the table rocks back and forth. If your fourth leg is a little short, tap the top of the leg with a hammer until the table stops rocking. If the fourth leg is too short, turn the table over and tap the bottom of the fourth leg. When the table sits flat, screw the leg into place.

Trimming the Table

Now you need to cover all the exposed plywood edges on the lower case with moulding or adhesive veneer tape. I used iron-on veneer tape to cover the plywood edges around the drawers, and ¼" × ³/₄" maple moulding for all the other edges. Attach the moulding with glue and brads, then sand its edges flush to your case.

To make the back look a little more interesting, I added a piece of moulding to make it look like the front (see photo 3 to see how I did this).

cutting list (inches): *asian coffee table*

No.	Item	Dimensions T W L	Material
1	Top	1" x 20" x 42"	P
4	Legs	1¾" x 1¾" x 16"	P
2	Case top & bottom	¾" x 15" x 30½"	Ply
3	Sides & divider	¾" x 6½" x 14¼"	Ply
1	Back	¾" x 6½" x 30½"	Ply
2	False drawer fronts	⅞" x 6⁷/₁₆" x 14"	P
2	Drawer fronts	½" x 6¼" x 13½"	B
4	Drawer sides	½" x 6¼" x 13⅜"	B
2	Drawer backs	½" x 5¾" x 13½"	B
2	Drawer bottoms	¼" x 13½" x 13⅛"	Ply
	Moulding	¼" x ¾" x 10'	P

P=Maple • Ply=Maple or birch ply • B=Baltic birch ply

cutting list (millimeters): *asian coffee table*

No.	Item	Dimensions T W L	Material
1	Top	25 x 508 x 1067	P
4	Legs	45 x 45 x 406	P
2	Case top & bottom	19 x 381 x 775	Ply
3	Sides & divider	19 x 165 x 362	Ply
1	Back	19 x 165 x 775	Ply
2	False drawer fronts	22 x 163 x 356	P
2	Drawer fronts	13 x 158 x 343	B
4	Drawer sides	13 x 158 x 340	B
2	Drawer backs	13 x 146 x 343	B
2	Drawer bottoms	6 x 343 x 333	Ply
	Moulding	6 x 19 x 3050	P

P=Maple • Ply=Maple or birch ply • B=Baltic birch ply

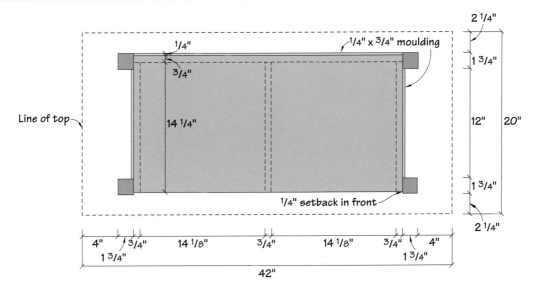

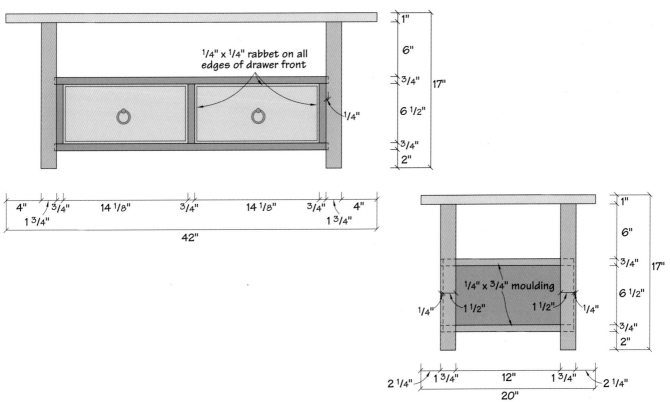

2 Getting the legs positioned so the table doesn't wobble is easiest to do before you screw the last leg in place (or you can spend a few hours cutting the legs with a hand saw after the table is completed; it's your choice). First clamp the fourth leg in place. Tap the top until the table sits flat. Screw the leg to the case.

3 You want the back of the coffee table to look as interesting as the front. To mimic the divider on the front of the case, I pinned a piece of moulding in the middle of the back, too.

4 Figure-eight fasteners are perfect for this project. Be sure to cut the recess for the fastener in the position shown so the hardware will move when the top moves.

Big Slab Top

Now trim your top to finished size, sand it and get ready to screw it to the table base. Your best bet is to use figure-eight fasteners. They are quick, sturdy and let your top expand and contract with the seasons. To install them, chuck a $\frac{3}{4}$" Forstner bit into your drill and cut a shallow hole in the top of the leg as shown in photo 4 at lower left. The depth of the hole should be the thickness of the fastener.

Screw the fasteners to the legs. Then turn your top upside down on a blanket and position the base upside down on the top. Drill pilot holes for the screws and then screw the top to the base.

Drawers

The drawers are simple plywood boxes with a solid maple drawer front screwed to the subfront. Here's how you make the plywood box. Cut your pieces to size. Then cut a $\frac{1}{4}$" × $\frac{1}{2}$"-wide rabbet on both ends of the sides. To hold the bottom in place, cut a $\frac{1}{4}$" × $\frac{1}{4}$" groove on the plywood front and sides that's $\frac{1}{4}$" up from the bottom edge. Nail and glue the plywood back and front between the side pieces. Slide the plywood bottom in place and nail it to the back.

Now prepare the maple drawer fronts. Cut a $\frac{1}{4}$" × $\frac{1}{4}$" rabbet on the front edges. It's a decorative detail that gives an extra shadow line around the drawers. Now screw the maple drawer fronts in place on the plywood boxes.

If you like your drawers to have a snug fit, attach a couple short pieces of veneer tape to the inside sides of the case. There's just enough space for a household iron.

Add a couple coats of clear finish and you're ready to load up your new coffee table with books, magazines and a cup of joe. ∎

dresser-top
VALET

For men, a jewelry box is unthinkable. Yet we still need a place to stow our stuff. This small-scale dresser-top box does the trick.

IT DOESN'T MATTER IF I'VE BEEN IN THE shop or at a swanky soiree. At the end of the day I empty the exact same contents of my pockets onto my dresser: wallet, knife, keys, change and watch.

Instead of keeping my manly necessities in one of my baseball caps, this valet seemed the perfect solution.

The cocobolo wood in this project priced out at $28 per board foot, so I had to be careful with it. My first step was to make sure I had enough material to resaw two ½"-thick pieces from a board.

Cocobolo is pretty stable, so there shouldn't be much movement after resawing.

Dish Out the Dividers

The next step is to make a template to rout the top. Lay out a full-size pattern from the diagram. Use ½" radii on the corners. The template for the top should be ½" Baltic birch. Make a copy of the pattern so you don't cut up the original. Paste the pattern down using spray mount or some other light adhesive. Don't worry about making sure the pattern is square to the board. You'll fix this after cutting out the holes. Rough cut the openings between the dividers. This is best done with a scroll saw. When you've finished the rough cutting, nail down guide strips (the exact same width as the dividers) right over the dividers in the pattern, and flush rout right up to the guides. After this is done, nail and glue guide strips to the back edge and one end of the pattern. When you place the top in the template, it will be square to the cutout holes. Always do a test piece on scrap plywood. With a core box bit in your router, set the depth of cut to ¼" beneath the template. A core box bit with a bearing on top will give nice-looking results on the edges. However, because the tip of the bit only touches the bottom of its cut, the bottom will look a little rough from moving the router back and forth. Try to remove as much material as possible with the router; then, after assembly, scrape the bottoms out with the homemade scraper described on the next page.

Make the Case

Once the other box parts are cut out, form a ¼" × ¼" rabbet on the bottom edges of the sides to capture the bottom. Mill a ¼"-

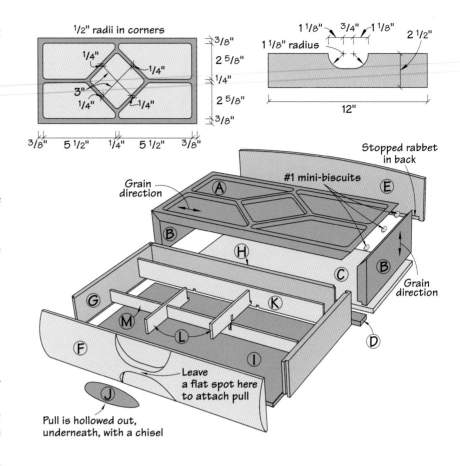

Pull is hollowed out, underneath, with a chisel

Leave a flat spot here to attach pull

thick bottom and glue a cocobolo front edge to it. The edge of the poplar bottom requires no prep before gluing, but the cocobolo does. One of the things you need to know about cocobolo is that it's an oily wood. Its oil content will actually weaken a standard wood glue joint, if not make it fail, over time. With the advent of polyurethane adhesives, this problem is basically eliminated. Simply wipe the cocobolo edges being glued with an oil-cutting

solvent such as lacquer thinner. Apply poly glue to one edge and moisten the other edge with water, to accelerate the curing of the glue. The same advice goes for the miters on the box. When the bottom is dry, rip it to finished size, which includes a stub that fits into a rabbet in the back.

Now cut the 45° miters on the box top and sides. Lay out and cut mini-biscuit slots in both ends of the joints. The other option is to use a spline in the miter. Just

cutting list (inches): *dresser-top valet*

No.	Ltr.	Item	Dimensions T W L	Material
1	A	Top	½" x 6¼" x 12"	P
2	B	Sides	½" x 6¼" x 2½"	P
1	C	Bottom	¼" x 5⅝" x 11½"	S
1	D	Bottom edge	¼" x ¾" x 11½"	P
1	E	Back	¼" x 3" x 12"	P
1	F	Drawer front	½" x 2½" x 12"	P
2	G	Drawer sides	¼" x 1¾" x 6⅜"	S
1	H	Drawer back	¼" x 1¾" x 10⅝"	S
1	I	Drawer bottom	¼" x 6¼" x 10⅝"	Plywood
1	J	Pull	½" x ⅝" x 3"	Ebony
1	K	Divider	⅛" x 1" x 10⅜"	S
2	L	Dividers	⅛" x ¾" x 3⅜"	S
1	M	Divider	⅛" x ⅝" x 10⅜"	S

P=Primary wood • S=Secondary wood, such as poplar

cutting list (millimeters): *dresser-top valet*

No.	Ltr.	Item	Dimensions T W L	Material
1	A	Top	13 x 58 x 305	P
2	B	Sides	13 x 58 x 64	P
1	C	Bottom	6 x 143 x 292	S
1	D	Bottom edge	6 x 19 x 292	P
1	E	Back	6 x 76 x 305	P
1	F	Drawer front	13 x 64 x 305	P
2	G	Drawer sides	6 x 45 x 162	S
1	H	Drawer back	6 x 45 x 289	S
1	I	Drawer bottom	6 x 158 x 289	Plywood
1	J	Pull	13 x 6 x 76	Ebony
1	K	Divider	3 x 25 x 264	S
2	L	Dividers	3 x 19 x 86	S
1	M	Divider	3 x 16 x 264	S

P=Primary wood • S=Secondary wood, such as poplar

be careful not to cut into the area where the routed depressions will be on the top. After preparing your joinery, including cutting the bottom to length, glue the box together with poly glue. Make sure the bottom is flush to the front. Because the open time on poly glue is pretty long (15 minutes or more), it's easy to get everything square. When the glue has cured, clean up the glue foam that squeezes out. Then rout the top depressions using your template, and clean the depressions with a small scraper. On the back, cut a stopped rabbet, $\frac{1}{4}" \times \frac{1}{8}"$ by the length of the bottom, and fit it to the bottom sticking out of the box. Cut a $48\frac{1}{4}"$ radius on the back. A simple way to create this redius is to bend a metal rule, touching both ends and the middle of the back's top edge. Draw a pencil line and saw off the waste. Clean up with a plane and glue the back in place.

Build the Drawer

I found the best way to get a great fit on the drawer is to cut the front oversize and mount the drawer parts to it. Make sure to joint a straight, square bottom edge on the front. Start from the middle and lay out the $\frac{1}{4}"$-deep mortises for the drawer sides and the groove for the bottom. Use a shop-built square to guide a small router with a $\frac{1}{8}"$ bit to cut the bottom groove first ($\frac{1}{4}"$ up from the bottom edge). The $\frac{1}{4}"$ thickness is nominal for birch plywood, so the groove will be closer to $\frac{3}{16}"$. Make two passes. Then cut the mortises for the sides. Cut a tongue-and-dado joint (as shown in the diagram on page 28) to hold the back between the sides. Then cut a $\frac{1}{8}"$ × $\frac{1}{8}"$ rabbet on the inside, bottom edge of the drawer sides and back to match up with the groove in the bottom. This rabbet holds the drawer bottom. When you're happy with the fit of all the drawer parts, glue them together and check your drawer for square.

After the drawer is dry, clean it up and cut the ends flush to the case. Plane the top flush if necessary. Now prepare to rout the two relief cuts on the top and bottom of the front. First cut a template to size according to the diagram. You need to cut the rounded shape on only one side of the template. You can flip the template over to rout the other side of the drawer front. Nail stops to the edge opposite the cutout

The template is made by rough cutting the holes and nailing guides to the lines over the dividers. Clean up the openings with a flush-cut router bit. When done, simply pry the guides off and you're in business.

and to the ends to index the template for routing. Rout the relief cuts.

Now form the curve on the drawer front. Make angled relief cuts to remove material on the top and bottom edges of the drawer front. Clamp the drawer in a vise and plane the radius on the front. Leave a small flat spot in the middle of the drawer front for attaching the pull. Cut the pull from a single piece of Gaboon ebony. Whittle and sand it to size and slightly undercut its bottom side. Attach it to the front with poly glue.

Make the drawer dividers from $\frac{1}{8}"$-thick maple and notch them together like an egg crate. When everything has been fit and sanded, apply three coats of clear Watco Danish Oil. After the finish has cured, mask off the internal drawer sides and use flocking to line the drawer bottom.

When done, place the dividers in the drawer and you're done. ∎

supplies

Woodcraft (800) 225-1153

- Black flocking, item# 6W43
- Black adhesive, item# 17H31
- Mini flocking gun, item# 127115

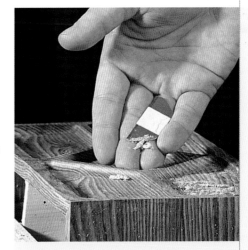

Scraper From the Joint

Taking a cue from some of the tricks used by prison inmates, I used utility knife blades with a ground edge on both bevels to make a serviceable, miniature scraper for the depressions on the drawer front and box top. Simply dull the cutting edge of the blade and grind the bevels square to the sides. Grind a roundover on the sharp corner to get into the $\frac{1}{4}"$ radius of the depressions. Wrap the middle with tape to keep a secure grip.

magic SHELVES

The magic of engineering, that is: Where ultra-light construction and a wall-attachment trick create a seamless illusion.

GO AHEAD. TAKE A GUESS. Just what do you think one of these shelf units weighs? I'll give you a hint. The thickness is 1⅜", the length of the longest leg is 78" with the other at 61". The height is 24", and the depth is 11". Some serious

cherry timbers, you think? Say 40 or 50 pounds? Well, guess again friend 'cause you're off by a factor of two. Yes, 23 pounds for the big unit and only 20 pounds for the smaller one.

Each shelf unit has three torsion boxes with solid cherry front edges, a top and bottom of ¼" cherry plywood and several pine ribs that run cross-grain to the cherry ply, or perpendicular to the front edge. It's all glued together to make a strong, flat and lightweight panel.

So how is it fixed to the wall? I'm not revealing that trick until the second act!

And by the way, if you think you've seen these shelves before, chances are you have. Our version was inspired by those shown in an Ace Hardware advertisement. I wasn't surprised to learn from Ace that they'd had hundreds of requests for plans to build this project. When I suggested we feature it here, they jumped at the chance.

Torsion (or Anti-Torsion) Boxes

Before heading to the shop, understand what you are essentially making are a series of torsion boxes. Now why they are called torsion boxes and not anti-torsion boxes I'll never know. To me, "torsion" means "twisted" or "twisting," and what this construction technique does is prevent that from happening. Things from aircraft wings and fuselages to hollow-core doors use this principle to keep their shape, even under a lot of stress. If you do much woodworking, you'll find torsion boxes a terrific solution to construction "problems" that come up from time to time.

After looking over the drawings and collecting your materials, begin by cutting the parts. Cut the plywood to length and width, then mill the solid cherry for the front edges. At this stage, leave the solid cherry a little long and keep the edges square, but cut the ½" × ¼" rabbet where the plywood will be joined to the solid front edge. You should make sure the rabbet's depth leaves the solid edge flush or just proud of the plywood.

Build the Ribs

Now cut the pieces you'll need to provide the buildup between the two plywood faces. It should be exactly the thickness of the dimension created by the two rabbet cuts. Note there are, however, two different widths and lengths. The pieces that are assembled at each end are both longer and wider than the intermediate ones. Lastly, cut out four strips of plastic laminate to the dimensions given. If you don't have a plas-

1 The shelf panel torsion box is made up of a solid cherry front edge, a top and bottom ¼" cherry plywood skin, and a series of built-up ribs. All the parts are glued together to make a strong, lightweight, torsion-resistant panel.

2 After gluing and pinning the cherry plywood skin to one side, flip the partial assembly and glue all the parts. Then pin together both sides. If you don't have a pinner, you can clamp all the parts, although this method should be done in several stages.

tic laminate such as Formica handy, you could substitute ¹⁄₁₆" × 1" precut strips of aluminum or steel.

Before starting assembly of the shelf panels, glue the plastic or metal strips to the inside back edge of the plywood that will be the top side of the four long shelves. This material will reinforce the plywood when you attach the shelves to

the wall. If you use plastic laminate, use either white or yellow woodworking glue. If you use metal, use an epoxy or polyurethane glue.

Panel Assembly

Depending on how your shop is equipped, assembly could go relatively quickly, or it could take a while. It'll be quick if you

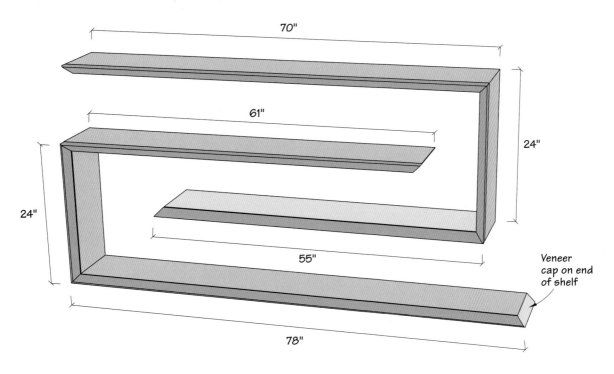

Veneer cap on end of shelf

cutting list (inches): *magic shelves*

No.	Item	Dimensions T W L	Material
2	Front edges	1³/₈" x 2" x 24"	Cherry
1	Front edge	1³/₈" x 2" x 78"	Cherry
1	Front edge	1³/₈" x 2" x 70"	Cherry
1	Front edge	1³/₈" x 2" x 61"	Cherry
1	Front edge	1³/₈" x 2" x 55"	Cherry
2	Shelf skins	¹/₄" x 9¹/₂" x 55⁵/₈"	Cherry ply
2	Shelf skins	¹/₄" x 9¹/₂" x 70⁵/₈"	Cherry ply
2	Shelf skins	¹/₄" x 9¹/₂" x 78⁵/₈"	Cherry ply
2	Shelf skins	¹/₄" x 9¹/₂" x 61⁵/₈"	Cherry ply
4	Shelf skins	¹/₄" x 9¹/₂" x 24⁵/₈"	Cherry ply
12	End bldups	⁷/₈" x 2¹/₂" x 9¹/₈"	Pine
30	Bldups	⁷/₈" x 1¹/₂" x 7⁵/₈"	Pine

Approximately 22' hardwood cleat material ⁵/₈" x 2¹/₈".

cutting list (millimeters): *magic shelves*

No.	Item	Dimensions T W L	Material
2	Front edges	35 x 51 x 610	Cherry
1	Front edge	35 x 51 x 1981	Cherry
1	Front edge	35 x 51 x 1778	Cherry
1	Front edge	35 x 51 x 1549	Cherry
1	Front edge	35 x 51 x 1397	Cherry
2	Shelf skins	6 x 242 x 1413	Cherry ply
2	Shelf skins	6 x 242 x 1794	Cherry ply
2	Shelf skins	6 x 242 x 1997	Cherry ply
2	Shelf skins	6 x 242 x 1565	Cherry ply
4	Shelf skins	6 x 242 x 626	Cherry ply
12	End bldups	22 x 67 x 232	Pine
30	Bldups	22 x 38 x 194	Pine

Approximately 6710mm hardwood cleat material 22mm x 54mm.

have a pneumatic pinner/nailer, slower if you have to rely on clamps exclusively. Regardless, the process will be the same.

First, glue one plywood piece to one of the rabbets in the cherry edge. Make sure you have a nice tight joint. For this, white or yellow glue is fine. Next, glue the end and intermediate ribs in place, spacing them about a foot apart. For this cross-grain gluing, use polyurethane glue. Also, use this glue where the end of each rib butts the solid cherry. Lastly, glue the second piece of plywood.

Even if you use a pneumatic pinner, clamp the ends and the rabbet joints. Also, keep your nails out of the way of the 45° end cuts to come later. Don't forget to pin or clamp the pine pieces on both sides of

the shelf.

Continue assembling panels until all four horizontal and two vertical panels are done.

After the glue has dried, sand or use a scraper to flush up the surfaces where the plywood and front edge meet. Now you are almost ready to cut the big chamfer on the front edge of each panel. Carefully mark each panel so that the reinforced plywood back edge is facing up for correct orientation to the chamfer. Next, use your router to form a ¹/₄" radius on what will be the outside of each panel's front edge. When done, cut the chamfer using your table saw so the cut blends into the radius detail.

The ends of each panel now get a

cross-grain miter cut. Again, before cutting, note the orientation of the cut relative to the reinforced plywood. It's best to put the three parts that make up one unit together, mark the edges to be glued later and — for the horizontal pieces — the end which is strictly decorative. Make the cut with a table saw, sliding compound miter saw or a radial arm saw.

The last bit of preparation before assembly is to cut biscuit joints in the miters that will be glued together.

Assembly

Dry-assemble the parts to check fittings and figure out a clamping strategy. I fashioned an I-beam-type gluing fixture out of ³/₄" plywood that 1) held the long panels

3 After the glue has cured and a ¼" radius has been routed on the correct long edge of the front, cut the big chamfer detail on the table saw.

4 Each of the six panels must be mitered on both ends. Take special care to make sure your cuts are properly oriented to the panels' final assembly positions.

up and in position while assembling; 2) gave me a surface to clamp to that didn't require long clamps; and 3) went a long way toward holding the entire assembly square during the process.

After the glue has set up and before removing the I-beam brace, make a simple support that attaches to the back side that will support the long "legs" through the rest of the work and until you install the units. Just make simple blocks that can be screwed into one of the interior pine pieces, then screw a brace between them.

Now cap the other long ends that are chamfered with some homemade cherry veneer. Slice four pieces that are about ¹⁄₁₆" thick from a piece of cherry of sufficient width. Size the pieces so that there is about ⅛" extra all around when applied. A simple way to attach these is to use contact cement. Trim and sand off the overhang after applying.

In preparation for installation, cut lengths of a sound hardwood, such as oak or maple, milled to the exact thickness of the opening in the back of each long shelf. The width should be about ⅛" less than the depth of the opening. These pieces will be securely fastened to the wall studs and positioned so that the openings in the rear of the shelves will sleeve over them. Screws will then be used to fasten each shelf to its wall cleat. You can predrill and countersink holes in the top rear edge of the shelf, spaced about 14" apart. (Now you understand why the plastic laminate or metal was used to reinforce the thin plywood.) Wait until you are ready to install the shelves before drilling pilot holes in the cleats. That way, you can mount the cleats on the wall, then position and mark the locations for pilot holes.

To complete the shop portion of this project, thoroughly sand the shelves and be careful to remove any dried glue, especially near the miter joints. Sand to 150 grit. For this project, I clear-coated the units with lacquer. Take the time to sand between coats to help achieve a nice, smooth finish.

Ultimately, this is a simple project that is a terrific primer on torsion box construction and produces a striking end result. You might say that, for all but the most novice of woodworkers, it's a project you can ace. ∎

5 The long panels are joined to the short vertical panels using biscuits in the miter joint. The biscuits strengthen the joint and help hold alignment during glue-up.

6 What could be an unwieldy glue-up is simplified using an I-beam-shaped plywood fixture. The fixture clamps to the long panels, holding them in place, provides a clamping surface for pulling the end in position and helps keep the whole assembly square.

7 The shelves hang on cleats that are carefully positioned and then screwed to the wall.

Detail of Shelf

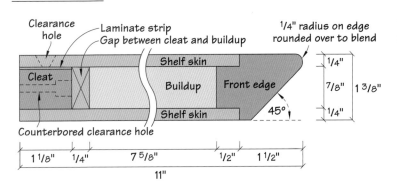

Clearance hole

Laminate strip
Gap between cleat and buildup

1/4" radius on edge rounded over to blend

Shelf skin

Cleat

Buildup   Front edge

1/4"
7/8"   1 3/8"
1/4"

Shelf skin   45°

Counterbored clearance hole

1 1/8"   1/4"   7 5/8"   1/2"   1 1/2"

11"

modern console

AS A WOODWORKER THERE IS A CERTAIN freedom in being able to design and build anything for yourself that you want. Sometimes you see a piece you like, and it sets your design juices flowing. Other times it takes only an amazing piece of wood or a really great-looking door handle to make you put pen to paper and start drawing. But the freedom is there. When you decide to turn your talents towards making a living, however, some of that freedom disappears. Now it's the customer's freedom you respond to. They see the piece of furniture or the door handle, not you. I consider myself lucky when a customer gets that urge, then turns to me to develop his or her "sighting" into a piece of furniture just for them.

That's how these shelving units were born. A customer showed up with a picture from an interior design magazine. He liked the way some shelves were spaced randomly and provided open space. The rest was up to me. Now that's a good customer. In a few days I had a sketch he liked. All I had to do then was figure out how to build it.

Slab Construction

To keep the shelving open, random and stout, I came up with the idea of gluing pieces of $\frac{3}{4}$"-thick plywood together to make $1\frac{1}{2}$"-thick slabs. I then cut $\frac{1}{2}$"-long tenons on the ends that fit into $\frac{1}{2}$"-deep grooves in the sides. Iron veneer tape to the exposed plywood edges, and the whole piece has a clean look and is stout as a bull.

To make the piece even more interesting, I added the "stubs" to make it appear that the shelves (and one partition) extend through the other piece.

A Slab of Ply

The upper shelving sections are 12" deep, have veneer-taped fronts and no back. This is a great size if you can find 49"-wide plywood, which isn't all that strange. If you can find only 48" ply, you may want to reduce your shelf width to $11\frac{3}{4}$".

Start by ripping the plywood into 12"-wide pieces. Each upper unit needs six 12" × 96" pieces, so if you're building two units you'll need three sheets, plus material for the lower units.

Glue the slabs together, trying to keep the edges as flush to one another as possible. A jointer pass on each long edge after the glue is dry should fix any inconsistencies, but more than that and the shelves won't be 12" deep.

Simple Dado Jig

With the slabs prepared, refer to the cutting list and cut the slabs to the lengths given. Note that the lengths include the $\frac{1}{2}$"-long tenons, so you won't have to add that to the dimensions for cutting. Separate all the pieces into piles that require dadoes, and with those that don't, use the diagrams to mark all the dado locations.

I built a simple jig to use with my plunge router to make cutting the dadoes quick and reasonably foolproof. Stop dadoes are necessary here, so I made a jig to hook over the back edge of the partition or shelf, and added a stop at the front of the jig set to stop my router $\frac{1}{4}$" from the front edge of the shelf. Dimensions for the jig are determined by the base on your router. Using a plunge router and a guide bushing, I was able to do each dado in two or three passes, lowering the depth of the router bit with each pass until I reached the full $\frac{1}{2}$" depth. The width of the tem-

1 With the dado locations laid out, clamp the jig in place and make a few passes with a router. Note that my jig was made from scraps of doubled-up ply. Yours doesn't need to be as stout.

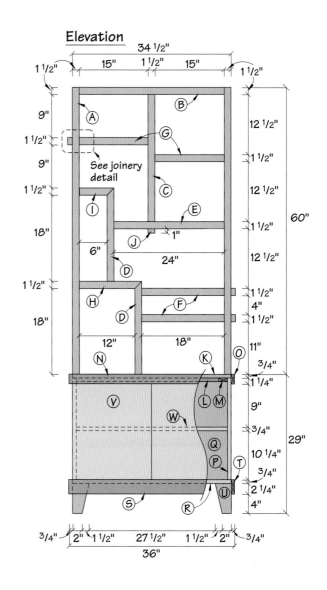

Elevation

2 The tenons are cut in two passes on each side to reduce the stress on the bit. Here I'm running the last pass on one of the stubs. I used a backing piece for all the passes to reduce chip-out.

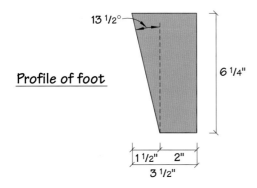

Profile of foot

13 1/2°

6 1/4"

1 1/2" 2"

3 1/2"

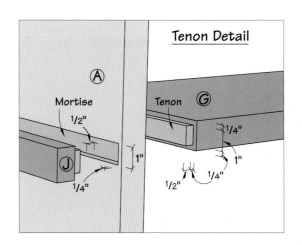

Tenon Detail

Mortise
1/2"
(J)
1/4"

Tenon (G)
1/4"
1"
1/2" 1/4"

(A)
1"

3 Fitting the tenons is extremely important as they hold the top section together. When assembled, the shelf and stub make it look like the shelf runs straight through the upright.

cutting list (inches): *modern console*

UPPER SHELVING (FOR ONE UNIT)

No.	Ltr.	Item	Dimensions T W L	Material	Comments
2	A	Sides	1½" x 12" x 60"	Plywood	
1	B	Top	1½" x 12" x 32½"	Plywood	½"TBE
1	C	Partition	1½" x 12" x 27½"	Plywood	½"TBE
2	D	Partitions	1½" x 12" x 20"	Plywood	½"TOE/MOE
1	E	Shelf	1½" x 12" x 25"	Plywood	½"TBE
2	F	Shelves	1½" x 12" x 19"	Plywood	½"TBE
2	G	Shelves	1½" x 12" x 16"	Plywood	½"TBE
1	H	Shelf	1½" x 12" x 14"	Plywood	½"TOE/MOE
1	I	Shelf	1½" x 12" x 8"	Plywood	½"TOE/MOE
4	J	Stubs	1½" x 12" x 1½"	Plywood	½"TOE

*Length includes tenons

LOWER CABINETS (FOR ONE UNIT)

No.	Ltr.	Item	Dimensions T W L	Material	Comments
1	K	Top	¾" x 17¼" x 34½"	Plywood	
1	L	Cleat	¾" x 1" x 34½"	Birch	
2	M	Cleats	¾" x 1" x 14½"	Birch	
1	N	Front edge	¾" x 2" x 36"	Birch	
2	O	Side edges	¾" x 2" x 18"	Birch	
2	P	Sides	¾" x 16½" x 20¼"	Plywood	
1	Q	Back	¾" x 33¼" x 21"	Plywood	
1	R	Bottom	¾" x 16½" x 34½"	Plywood	
2	S	Long edges	¾" x 3" x 36"	Birch	
2	T	Side edges	¾" x 3" x 18"	Birch	
4	U	Feet	3½" x 3½" x 6¼"	Birch	
2	V	Doors	¾" x 17⅛" x 20"	Plywood	
1	W	Shelf	¾" x 15½" x 33"	Plywood	Use shelf pins

TBE= tenon on both ends • TOE=tenon on one end • MOE=miter on one end

plate was set to allow a 1"-wide dado. The rest is routing.

Tenon Time

After the dadoes are completed, cut tenons on the appropriate ends. Use your router table with a two-pass process. Set the router fence to take a ¼" × ¼" pass for the first cut. Run both sides of each tenoned end, then reset the fence for ¼" × ½" and run the pieces again. Make sure you cut a test piece or two to get the best fit in the dadoes. This mechanical joint and some glue are the only things holding the upper section together.

To make the tenons blind, use this same setup to run the shorter pieces on edge through the router table. The longer pieces need to be cut by hand for safety.

Some of the pieces meet at a miter joint. I used a ¼" × 1½" × 11" spline at each miter, cutting the groove with a slot cutter in my router. Four No. 20 biscuits at each miter would also work well.

Veneer Tape and Clamps

You're now ready to fire up your iron and do some veneer edge taping. 2"-wide veneer tape isn't cheap, but if you compare it to the cost of solid lumber, you'll find it a bargain.

With the edges taped, it's time to see how many clamps you own. The upper assemblies are difficult to glue at one time, so glue and clamp them in sections.

Start with one side, and glue the pieces together to form the two 12½" × 15" upper sections (B, C, E and G) to that side. As a next step (or at the same time if you've got the clamps) glue the two 19" shelf pieces (F) to the side, and the mitered 20" piece (D) to them.

Next, glue the mitered pieces that form the 6" × 18" space (D, H and I) to the other side piece. Now glue the two sides together, adding the top piece and the last shelf at this time. Lastly, glue the stubs in place.

After every clamping step, check your work for square. It doesn't take much to

throw off the next step and make the whole finished piece looked wopperjawed.

The Lower Cabinet

The base unit uses fairly simple construction, but I used bookmatched veneer on the doors for a dramatic effect. If you purchase your plywood carefully you might be able to find good veneer patterns without having to actually veneer the doors. I wasn't that lucky.

The cabinet is simply two plywood sides with ½" × ¾" rabbeted back edges to capture a ¾"-thick back. I chose a thick back for three reasons: One, it added support for the weight of the upper unit. Two, it made the lower cabinet stronger overall. And three, it allowed me to cut ventilation slots through the back for electronic components without affecting the structural support.

Start by building the base. Cut the bottom piece to size, then cut, miter and glue the 3"-wide solid birch edging to the front, back and both sides of the bottom piece,

cutting list (millimeters): *modern console*

UPPER SHELVING (FOR ONE UNIT)

No.	Ltr.	Item	Dimensions T W L	Material	Comments
2	A	Sides	38 x 305 x 1524	Plywood	
1	B	Top	38 x 305 x 826	Plywood	13mmTBE
1	C	Partition	38 x 305 x 699	Plywood	13mmTBE
2	D	Partitions	38 x 305 x 508	Plywood	13mmTOE/MOE
1	E	Shelf	38 x 305 x 635	Plywood	13mmTBE
2	F	Shelves	38 x 305 x 483	Plywood	13mmTBE
2	G	Shelves	38 x 305 x 406	Plywood	13mmTBE
1	H	Shelf	38 x 305 x 356	Plywood	13mmTOE/MOE
1	I	Shelf	38 x 305 x 203	Plywood	13mmTOE/MOE
4	J	Stubs	38 x 305 x 38	Plywood	13mmTOE

*Length includes tenons

LOWER CABINETS (FOR ONE UNIT)

No.	Ltr.	Item	Dimensions T W L	Material	Comments
1	K	Top	19 x 438 x 877	Plywood	
1	L	Cleat	19 x 25 x 877	Birch	
2	M	Cleats	19 x 25 x 369	Birch	
1	N	Front edge	19 x 51 x 914	Birch	
2	O	Side edges	19 x 51 x 457	Birch	
2	P	Sides	19 x 419 x 514	Plywood	
1	Q	Back	19 x 844 x 533	Plywood	
1	R	Bottom	19 x 419 x 877	Plywood	
2	S	Long edges	19 x 76 x 914	Birch	
2	T	Side edges	19 x 76 x 457	Birch	
4	U	Feet	89 x 89 x 158	Birch	
2	V	Doors	19 x 435 x 508	Plywood	
1	W	Shelf	19 x 394 x 838	Plywood	Use shelf pins

TBE= tenon on both ends • TOE=tenon on one end • MOE=miter on one end

4 With all the dadoes and tenons run, the next step is veneer tape. Buy big rolls and save money.

holding the edging flush to the top edge of the bottom.

Next, veneer the front edges of the two sides, then mark the location of the sides on the bottom (holding the sides flush to the back edge of the bottom) 1" in from each side. Drill 3/16" clearance holes through the bottom, then screw the sides in place, using the back to confirm the spacing. Then attach the back to hold the sides in place.

The top is made much like the bottom, with solid birch edges mitered and glued in place to the plywood top. But since it's unattractive to put screws through the top, add 3/4" × 1" cleats to the top edges of the sides and back. The top shelving is attached by screwing up through the cleats into the top.

To raise the cabinets off the ground I made solid feet, beveled on two sides, and doweled them into the underside of the bottom. I used a solid piece of wood because I had it handy, but you could also make two-sided corners from 3/4"-thick

material that would mimic the look of solid feet.

Except for shelving that you may want in the cabinets, the doors are the last pieces. Again, choose the look you want for the front of the doors, then add veneer tape to the edges. I used free-swinging European hinges to mount the doors, and added touch latches to the doors to avoid using pulls.

With a couple of coats of clear lacquer, the cabinets were ready to deliver. My customer was delighted to see his image turned into reality, and I was happy to keep an easy-to-work-with customer happy. ∎

supplies

Constantine's, www.constanines.com (954) 561-1716

• 1 - 2" x 250' (51mm x 76.25m) roll of iron-on birch veneer edge tape, item# K222 $83.00, or 2" x 8' (51mm x 2.4m) strips, item# WE13, $5.25 per strip (6 required)
• 1 - 1 3/16" x 50' (21mm x 15.25m) roll of iron-on birch veneer edge tape, item #K522, $12.45

Constantine's also offers veneer tape for this project in red oak, white oak, mahogany or walnut. Prices will vary.

step
Tansu

The traditional cabinetry of Japan is simple, stylish and sturdy.

THE HARD MAPLE GRAIN PATTERN REMINDS me of the ink landscapes drawn by Chinese and Japanese artists beginning in A.D. 700. Each painting, with its jagged mountains and forbidding peaks, was supposed to represent a little story. The viewer followed people travelling on a path through the painting. So when I decided to build a step tansu, the obvious choice was maple, despite the fact that these chests were traditionally built from Japanese cypress, cedar or elm.

"Tansu" means chest, and the high period of this type of furniture was 1657 to 1923. The traditional Japanese household would store clothing, valuables and household items in its tansu.

CONSTRUCTION OF THIS CHEST is simple. You'll need a sheet and a half of ¾" maple plywood, one board of 1"-thick maple that's about 8' long and 8" wide and some ½" and ¼" plywood scraps for the drawers. The carcasses of the upper and lower cabinets are built the same way. First cut all your pieces to size and iron on veneer edge tape to cover all the exposed plywood edges.

Now cut the grooves and rabbets on the cabinet stiles. The side panels are glued into ½"-deep by ¾"-wide grooves milled ¼" in from the edge of the cabinet stiles. The back panel is nailed and glued into a ½"-deep by ¾"-wide rabbet on the inside of the stiles. Screw each assembly to its bottom board. Glue and nail the partitions in place.

Lower Cabinet Doors

Build the two sliding doors using stub tenons that rest in ¼"-wide by ½"-deep grooves. The only exception to this is the grooves in the thin rails, which should be ¼"-wide and ¼"-deep. Also, the interior stiles are merely applied to the doors after construction; they are not structural. After dry-assembling your doors, glue and clamp them.

When dry, glue the interior stiles in place, and cut a ¼"-wide by ½"-deep groove on the top and bottom of each door that will allow the door to slide on the runners. Then cut the four runners; make sure they slide smoothly in the doors' grooves. Attach the runners to the top and bottom of the lower cabinet using brads and glue.

I spaced my runners so that the front door is flush to the front edge of the cabinet stiles. Then I left a ¹⁄₁₆" gap between

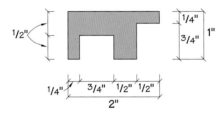

Detail of back cabinet stiles

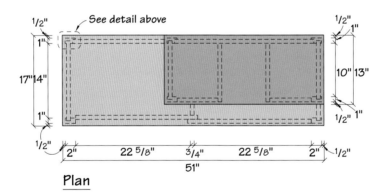

Plan

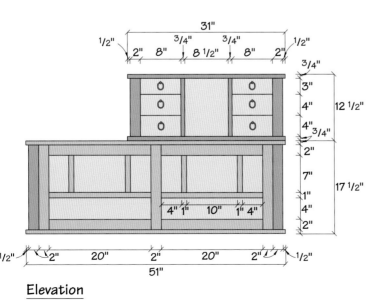

Elevation

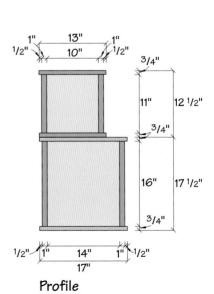

Profile

cutting list (inches): *step tansu*

LOWER CABINET

No.	Item	Dimensions T W L	Material
2	Top & Bottom	$3/4$" x 17" x 51"	Ply
4	Cabinet stiles	1" x 2" x 16"	M
2	Side panels	$3/4$" x 15" x 16"	Ply
1	Back panel	$3/4$" x 16" x 47"	Ply
4	Door stiles	$3/4$" x 2" x 16"	M
4	Door rails	$3/4$" x 2" x 21"	M
2	Thin rails	$3/4$" x 1" x 21"	M
2	Top panels	$1/4$" x $7^{11}/_{16}$" x 21"	Ply
2	Lower panels	$1/4$" x $4^{11}/_{16}$" x 21"	Ply
4	Interior stiles	$1/4$" x 1" x 7"	M
4	Runners	$1/4$" x $1/4$" x 46"	M
1	Partition	$3/4$" x 13" x 16"	Ply
3	Cleats	$3/4$" x $3/4$" x 13"	M

UPPER CABINET

No.	Item	Dimensions T W L	Material
2	Top & Bottom	$3/4$" x 13" x 31"	Ply
4	Cabinet stiles	1" x 2" x 11"	M
2	Side panels	$3/4$" x 11" x 11"	Ply
1	Back panel	$3/4$" x 11" x 27"	Ply
2	Vertical dividers	$3/4$" x $10^{1}/_{2}$" x 11"	Ply
4	Lg drawer fronts	$3/4$" x 4" x 8"	M
8	Drawer sides	$1/2$" x 4" x $10^{1}/_{8}$"	Ply
4	Drawer backs	$1/2$" x 4" x $7^{1}/_{2}$"	Ply
6	Drawer bottoms	$1/4$" x $7^{1}/_{2}$" x $9^{3}/_{4}$"	Ply
2	Sm drawer fronts	$3/4$" x 3" x 8"	M
2	Drawer sides	$1/2$" x 3" x $10^{1}/_{8}$"	Ply
4	Drawer backs	$1/2$" x 3" x $7^{1}/_{2}$"	Ply

M= Hard maple, Ply= Maple plywood

cutting list (millimeters): *step tansu*

LOWER CABINET

No.	Item	Dimensions T W L	Material
2	Top & Bottom	19 x 432 x 1295	Ply
4	Cabinet stiles	25 x 51 x 406	M
2	Side panels	19 x 381 x 406	Ply
1	Back panel	19 x 406 x 1194	Ply
4	Door stiles	19 x 51 x 406	M
4	Door rails	19 x 51 x 533	M
2	Thin rails	19 x 25 x 533	M
2	Top panels	6 x 196 x 533	Ply
2	Lower panels	6 x 120 x 533	Ply
4	Interior stiles	6 x 25 x 178	M
4	Runners	6 x 6 x 1168	M
1	Partition	19 x 330 x 406	Ply
3	Cleats	19 x 19 x 330	M

UPPER CABINET

No.	Item	Dimensions T W L	Material
2	Top & Bottom	19 x 330 x 787	Ply
4	Cabinet stiles	25 x 51 x 279	M
2	Side panels	19 x 279 x 279	Ply
1	Back panel	19 x 279 x 686	Ply
2	Vertical dividers	19 x 267 x 279	Ply
4	Lg drawer fronts	19 x 102 x 203	M
8	Drawer sides	13 x 102 x 257	Ply
4	Drawer backs	13 x 102 x 191	Ply
6	Drawer bottoms	6 x 191 x 248	Ply
2	Sm drawer fronts	19 x 76 x 203	M
2	Drawer sides	13 x 76 x 257	Ply
4	Drawer backs	13 x 76 x 191	Ply

M= Hard maple, Ply= Maple plywood

the two doors. Fit the doors to the opening in the chest. Now screw the top to the carcass through cleats that are screwed to the sides and partition of the case.

Upper Cabinet Drawers

Here's how to build the drawers: Cut $1/2$" × $3/8$" rabbets on the ends of the drawer fronts. Then cut $1/2$" × $1/4$" rabbets on the back edge of the sides to hold the back piece. Then cut a $1/4$" × $1/4$" groove to hold the drawer bottom on the sides, back and front that's $1/4$" up from the bottom edge. Glue and nail the sides to the drawer front. Slip the bottom in place. Glue and nail the back to the sides.

How you hang the drawers is up to you. I cut $1/4$"-deep by $5/8$"-wide stopped dadoes that were centered on each side of the drawer. Then I nailed drawer runners to the carcass's partitions and drawer runners with plywood build-up strips to the sides. When the drawers move smoothly, nail the top to the case. Putty any nail holes; apply three coats of a clear finish.

You might have noticed from the photo that I made the grain direction of the drawers run vertically instead of horizontally. This is OK for such small drawers, and I did this because each bank of drawers now reminds me of one of those Japanese landscape paintings. ■

supplies

**Misugi Designs, www.misugidesigns.com
(707) 422-0734**
• 6 Ryusen pulls, $6.80 each

closet
OVERHAUL

A few sheets of plywood and a weekend are all you need to promote marital harmony.

IF YOU LIKE FISHING, YOU'RE GOING TO like this project. You see, while a good deal of my business is building custom furniture and cabinets, a lot of my clients have asked me to revamp their closets. I've gotten pretty good at it. So good, in fact, that my wife, Terri, asked me to customize her closet. What does this have to do with fishing? Well, once I installed these new shelves and brackets, Terri was so happy she insisted I relax after that tough job (wink, wink) and go fishing in Canada.

Here's my wife's closet before I remodeled and put in the custom closet interior. There was a lot of wasted space in the old closet.

ADDING ADJUSTABLE SHELVES and extra hanging rods in your closet will typically give you at least 30 percent more space. And you don't need a lot of tools or materials to do the job right. I customized Terri's closet with only three sheets of plywood (plus a few scraps I had lying around) and some iron-on edge tape. The closet measured 26" deep, 78" wide and 100" high, which is pretty typical. You can adjust the shelves and hanger boards to fit your space.

Construction is not complicated. There are two hanger boards screwed to the studs on the back walls of the closet. One near the baseboard, and one near the ceiling. The tall sides are notched around these hanger boards and screwed into the hanger boards and top shelf. Then you install the adjustable shelves and hang rods. Done. Here's how to make this process go as quickly as possible.

Preparation Is Key

The more fussing you do before the installation, the quicker the whole process will go. Begin by cutting the plywood to size. I've included my materials list so you can adapt it for your closet. Start by working on the hanger boards. First cut the dadoes and rabbets that will hold the sides in place. It's easier to cut the dadoes and rabbets on a wider piece of ply and then rip the two hanger boards from that piece.

Cut a $\frac{1}{4}$"-deep by $\frac{3}{4}$"-wide rabbet on the end of each hanger board. Then cut $\frac{1}{4}$"-deep by $\frac{3}{4}$"-wide dadoes at the intervals you've decided are best for your closet. I have one small section of shelves with dadoes that are $15\frac{7}{8}$" apart. The larger shelves use dadoes that are $34\frac{7}{8}$" apart. And the dadoes for the section with the hanging rods are 24" apart. After cutting your dadoes, rip the two hanger boards from that piece.

Next turn to the side pieces. First cut the $\frac{1}{4}$"-deep by 3"-long notches on the back edge of each side. Now drill all your shelf pin holes using a shop-made or commercial jig. I drilled 5mm holes every 1" that were $1\frac{1}{4}$" in from the back and front edge. When you're drilling shelf pin holes on both faces of a piece of plywood, be sure to offset the holes a tad on one face. Otherwise you might end up drilling holes all the way through and your shelf pins will

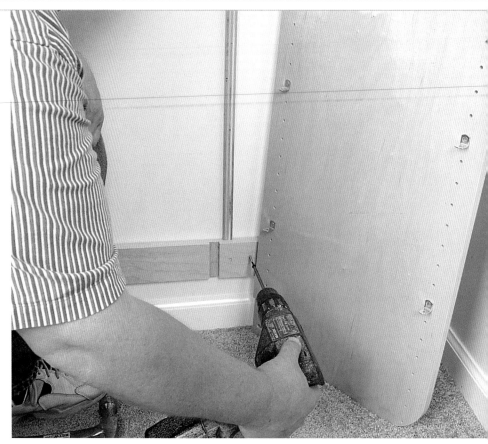

1 Attach the hanger boards to the wall with screws that are at least $2\frac{1}{2}$" long. Here you can see how all the shelf pins are in place before I began the installation.

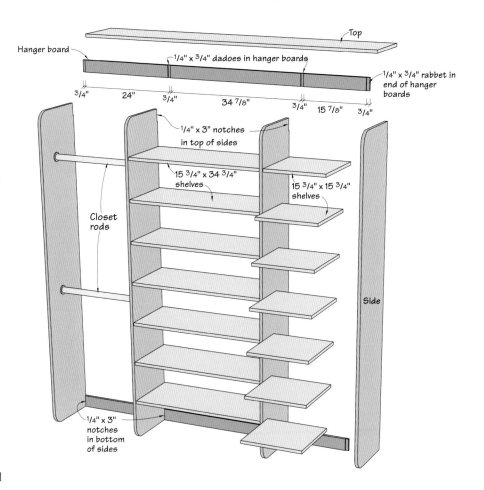

Hanger board

Top

$\frac{1}{4}$" x $\frac{3}{4}$" dadoes in hanger boards

$\frac{1}{4}$" x $\frac{3}{4}$" rabbet in end of hanger boards

$\frac{3}{4}$" 24" $\frac{3}{4}$" $34\frac{7}{8}$" $\frac{3}{4}$" $15\frac{7}{8}$" $\frac{3}{4}$"

$\frac{1}{4}$" x 3" notches in top of sides

$15\frac{3}{4}$" x $34\frac{3}{4}$" shelves

$15\frac{3}{4}$" x $15\frac{3}{4}$" shelves

Closet rods

Side

$\frac{1}{4}$" x 3" notches in bottom of sides

cutting list (inches): *closet overhaul*

No.	Item	Dimensions T W L	Material
4	Sides	$^3/_4$" x 15$^3/_4$" x 80"	BP
2	Hanger boards	$^3/_4$" x 3" x 77$^3/_4$"	BP
1	Top	$^3/_4$" x 12$^1/_4$" x 78"	BP
7	Small shelves	$^3/_4$" x 15$^3/_4$" x 15$^3/_4$"	BP
7	Large shelves	$^3/_4$" x 15$^3/_4$" x 34$^3/_4$"	BP

BP = Birch plywood

cutting list (millimeters): *closet overhaul*

No.	Item	Dimensions T W L	Material
4	Sides	19 x 400 x 2032	BP
2	Hanger boards	19 x 76 x 1969	BP
1	Top	19 x 311 x 1981	BP
7	Small shelves	19 x 400 x 400	BP
7	Large shelves	19 x 400 x 883	BP

BP = Birch plywood

2 Fit the sides into the rabbets and dadoes in your hanger boards. You can see the pocket holes I predrilled to attach the sides, top and hanger boards. I've found this method to be fast and reliable.

3 Make sure you check for square before you screw the sides to the top. If you don't, it will throw everything off, guaranteed.

hit each other. Now cut pocket holes to screw the sides to the hanger boards and the top shelf. I use a commercial jig. Cut a 3" radius on the top and bottom of the front edge with a router and a pattern. Iron edge tape to the plywood edges that show on the sides and shelves. Add a clear finish to all the parts.

Now install the brackets that hold the hanging rods. I put one 36" up from the bottom and another 77" from the bottom. It's easier to install these brackets now before you start screwing all the parts together.

Finally, put your shelf pins in. I know

this sounds odd, but after doing this for years I've found it much easier to do this before the installation when you can easily line up everything.

Installation Time

First install the hanger boards. Find the studs in the closet and screw the bottom hanger board to at least four of them. Then use a piece of scrap that's exactly as long as the space between the two notches on the side pieces to position the top hanger. Screw it into the studs.

Now attach the side pieces into the dadoes and rabbets in the hanger boards.

You'll notice that this arrangement leaves a bit of space between the wall and sides. This allows you to get electrical cords behind the sides in case you ever want to conceal a stereo or TV in your closet, and leaves a gap for any bows in your walls.

Now put the top shelf in place and screw the sides to the top. You're almost finished. Put the adjustable shelves in and pop the hanging rods into place.

Now splash some water on your face (you want to make it look like it was a lot of hard work), and tell your spouse you're done with the closet.

Fishing hole here I come. ∎

side
TABLE

By changing a couple of dimensions, this side table becomes a sofa table.

By lengthening the long aprons and the top, the side table design becomes a perfect sofa table.

THIS DESIGN HAS BECOME A STAPLE OF MY business, and I'm almost embarrassed to admit that some of its details started as mistakes. The bow-tie apron started out as an apron with a chevron cut on the underside. One day I wasn't paying attention and marked the chevron on both sides of the apron. I stopped, looked at the piece, and said, "Why not?"

Sometimes the best work is the adaptation of a fortuitous accident.

These simple tables use mortise-and-tenon joints for strength and a mechanical fastener to attach the top. In fact, these tables are so simple, you could build them with a jigsaw, hand plane, chisels and hammer.

There isn't all that much wood invested in the project, so it's a great opportunity to experiment with some exotic woods. I chose wenge (say "wen-gee") and zebrawood, which creates a sleek and stylish side table. And by changing a couple of dimensions, it's easy to produce a sofa table. Choose either or both table designs and follow the instructions to create your own work of art.

Making the Legs

Start the project by roughing the legs, aprons and top to size, then mark and cut the $\frac{3}{8}" \times 1" \times \frac{5}{8}"$-deep mortises on the two inside faces of each leg. The mortises are positioned to hold the top edge of the aprons $\frac{1}{8}"$ down from the rabbet cut on the leg. This also puts the outer face of the apron $\frac{1}{8}"$ in from the outside of the leg. Next cut the $\frac{3}{8}" \times 1" \times \frac{1}{2}"$-long tenons centered on the ends of the four aprons. While I mentioned this project could be completed with minimal tools, a table saw is useful for the tenoning.

The next step is possible with a jigsaw and chisel, but I used a router table to cut a $\frac{1}{4}" \times \frac{1}{4}"$ rabbet on the two top outside faces of all the legs. This detail gives a "floating" appearance to the top of the table.

With the rabbets cut, use a $\frac{1}{2}"$ Forstner bit to drill a $\frac{1}{8}"$ recess on the inside corner of each leg top. This recess hides a simple figure-eight top fastener and provides a strong assembly, while allowing the solid top to expand and contract during seasonal wood movement. If a Forstner bit isn't part of your tool collection, a chisel can be used to remove enough material to fit the fastener.

Now taper the two inside faces of each leg using a tapering jig on the table saw. The taper starts 3" down from the top of the leg and tapers to leave a $\frac{3}{4}" \times \frac{3}{4}"$ foot. No table saw or tapering jig? It's a lot more work, but a smoothing plane can create the same taper.

Cut the Aprons

Turning to the aprons, mark the bowtie shape on one face of each apron. The bowtie starts full-width at either end of the apron and tapers to $\frac{5}{8}"$ wide in the center. After marking the shape, use a band saw to

1 The two rabbets on the top of the leg add a simple but classy detail to the table. Use a sharp router bit and back the leg with a piece of scrap to guard against blowout.

2 A tapering jig makes this step fairly cut-and-dried, but don't get so comfortable that you don't pay attention to which face the mortises are on. It's easy to taper the wrong face.

cutting list (inches): *side table*

No.	Ltr.	Item	Dimensions T W L	Material
4	A	Legs	$1\frac{1}{4}" \times 1\frac{1}{4}" \times 33\frac{1}{4}"$	Wenge
4	B	Aprons	$\frac{3}{4}" \times 1\frac{1}{2}" \times 12\frac{1}{2}"$	Zebrawood
1	C	Top	$\frac{3}{4}" \times 14" \times 14"$	Zebrawood

FOR OPTIONAL SOFA TABLE:

No.	Item	Dimensions T W L	Material
4	Legs	$\frac{1}{4}" \times 1\frac{1}{4}" \times 33\frac{1}{4}"$	Wenge
2	Aprons	$\frac{3}{4}" \times 1\frac{1}{2}" \times 12\frac{1}{2}"$	Zebrawood
2	Long Aprons	$\frac{3}{4}" \times 1\frac{1}{2}" \times 47\frac{1}{2}"$	Zebrawood
1	Top	$\frac{3}{4}" \times 14" \times 49"$	Zebrawood

cutting list (millimeters): *side table*

No.	Ltr.	Item	Dimensions T W L	Material
4	A	Legs	32 x 32 x 844	Wenge
4	B	Aprons	19 x 38 x 318	Zebrawood
1	C	Top	19 x 356 x 356	Zebrawood

FOR OPTIONAL SOFA TABLE:

No.	Item	Dimensions T W L	Material
4	Legs	32 x 32 x 844	Wenge
2	Aprons	19 x 38 x 318	Zebrawood
2	Long Aprons	19 x 38 x 1207	Zebrawood
1	Top	19 x 356 x 1245	Zebrawood

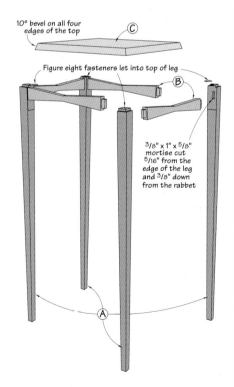

4 With the milling finished, the details of the corner joint come together in a pleasant mating of exotic woods using simple joinery.

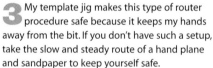

3 My template jig makes this type of router procedure safe because it keeps my hands away from the bit. If you don't have such a setup, take the slow and steady route of a hand plane and sandpaper to keep yourself safe.

cut each apron to shape. Cut to the outside of the line to allow a little material to clean up with a router or hand plane.

Again opting for a power tool here, I made a simple pattern template jig to hold each apron as I used a straight pattern-bearing bit to clean up the edges of each apron. The pattern jig makes sense for me because I make so many of these tables, but the edge can be cleaned up with a plane and some sanding.

Assemble the Base

At this point there are only a couple details to take care of before assembly. Finish sanding all the table pieces, gently breaking the edges and corners to leave most of the edges crisp. To add another simple detail, you can plane a ¹⁄₁₆" flat on the outside corner edge of each leg. The base is ready to glue and assemble.

5 A simple figure-eight fastener is used to attach the top and allows wood movement without damaging the base (left).

Make the Top

While the base is drying, determine the upper face of your top and use the table saw to cut a 10° bevel on the edges of the top to give a sloping plateau appearance. Then finish sanding the top and you're ready to put a clear finish on the piece and assemble.

Once you realize how simple this table is to create, try not to tell all your friends and relatives, or they'll be begging you to make one for them. ∎

10° bevel on all four edges of the top — Ⓒ

Figure eight fasteners let into top of leg — Ⓑ

³⁄₈" x 1" x ⁵⁄₈" mortise cut ⁵⁄₁₆" from the edge of the leg and ³⁄₈" down from the rabbet

Ⓐ

contemporary SHELVES

This simple plywood unit would look at home in a Soho loft or suburban great room. Special knockdown hardware makes it a snap to build.

IT'S RARE THAT BOOKSHELVES LOOK AS interesting as the objects you display. After all, how much can you decorate the shelves themselves? This unit is unusual because the shelves and sides are beefier than you would normally see, and the two bevel cuts on the front edges give these shelves nice visual interest.

Best of all, perhaps, is that this piece is simple and quick to build.

Dividers and Shelves

Start by cutting out the sides and shelves. The 1½"-thick sides are made by gluing two pieces of ¾"-thick plywood together. The 1¼"-thick shelves are made by gluing ¾"-thick plywood to a ½"-thick piece. Note that the finished sides have a ¾" × ¼" rabbet for the back that's formed by gluing a narrower piece to a wider one. The adjustable and fixed shelves in the side openings are all the same width. The center shelves are ¼" wider to account for the lack of a back.

To cut the sides, crosscut a whole sheet of plywood to the length of the sides, then rip them to width (11" and 11¼"). Cut the sides a little wide (¹⁄₁₆") to give yourself a little room to cut a square, straight edge. This will give you a clean edge for attaching a piece of maple later. Now nail and glue the dividers together, remembering to offset the back edge for the rabbet. Place your nails so the shelves will hide them.

Here's an easy way to cut the shelves. Rip them to width from a full piece of plywood, then nail and glue a length of shelving. Then crosscut the shelves to length from the long pieces. You can get five 16" shelves out of a 96" rip. For even less work, cut the shelves to length after attaching the edging.

Edges and Angles

The edges for the bookshelves are solid maple. Because the thicknesses of ¾" and ½" plywood is considered "nominal," you will end up with finished shelf thicknesses about ¹⁄₁₆" less. Rip your edging stock a little wide and attach it with biscuits and glue. With a flush-cut bearing bit in a router, trim the edging flush to the sides and shelves, then clean up your work with a plane or scraper.

The last step is to bevel the edging. Photo 2 shows how I did this on the table saw. Remember that the setup must change for the different width pieces.

Making it a Stand-Up Unit

The next step is to mill stopped grooves in the topmost and bottommost shelves to accept the tapered sliding connectors that attach the sides together. The grooves in the ends of the shelves are ¾" wide by approximately ⅜" deep, and milled with a dado set on the table saw. It helps to make

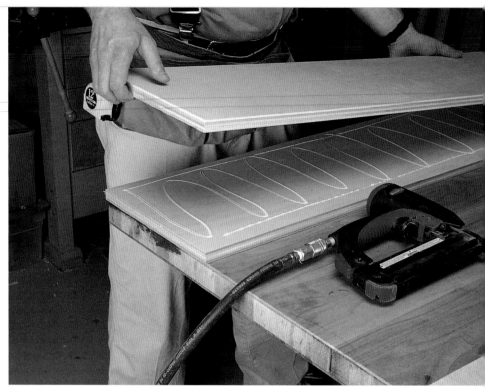

1 Once you've got your parts cut to size, glue and nail them together leaving the rabbet at the back. Set and putty the nails, then rip the dividers to their final width.

cutting list (inches): *contemporary shelves*

No.	Item	Dimensions T W L	Material
4	Sides	¾" × 11¼" × 84"	Plywood
4	Sides	¾" × 11" × 84"	Plywood
10	Outer shelf tops	¾" × 10⅛" × 16"	Plywood
10	Outer shelf bottoms	½" × 10⅛" × 16"	Plywood
5	Center shelf tops	¾" × 10⅜" × 16"	Plywood
5	Center shelf bottoms	½" × 10⅜" × 16"	Plywood
2	Backs	¼" × 17½" × 76"	Plywood
3	Aprons	¾" × 4" × 16"	Plywood
4	Side edging	¾" × 1½" × 84"	Maple
15	Shelf edging	¾" × 1¼" × 16"	Maple

cutting list (millimeters): *contemporary shelves*

No.	Item	Dimensions T W L	Material
4	Sides	19 × 285 × 2134	Plywood
4	Sides	19 × 279 × 2134	Plywood
10	Outer shelf tops	19 × 257 × 406	Plywood
10	Outer shelf bottoms	13 × 257 × 406	Plywood
5	Center shelf tops	19 × 264 × 406	Plywood
5	Center shelf bottoms	13 × 264 × 406	Plywood
2	Backs	6 × 445 × 1930	Plywood
3	Aprons	19 × 102 × 406	Plywood
4	Side edging	19 × 38 × 2134	Maple
15	Shelf edging	19 × 32 × 406	Maple

supplies

Woodworkers' Supply, (800) 645-9292
- 2-6" (152mm) taper connectors, item# 928273, $4.95/pkg. of four
- 18 wire shelf supports, item# 826028, $1.45 each for 10+

2 The bevels on the edges are basically a V shape on the entire edge. See the diagram for details and cutting angles. Clean up your saw marks with a plane.

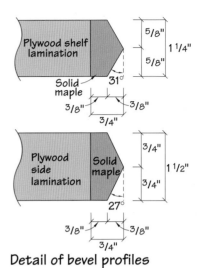

Detail of bevel profiles

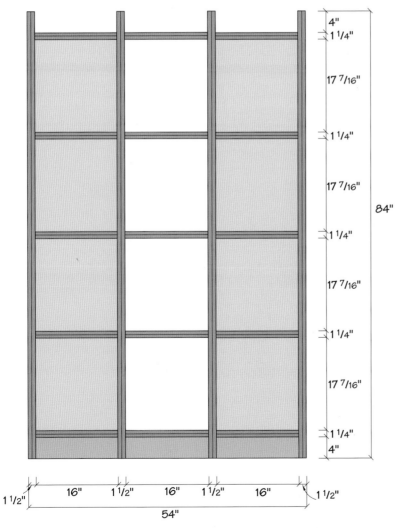

Elevation

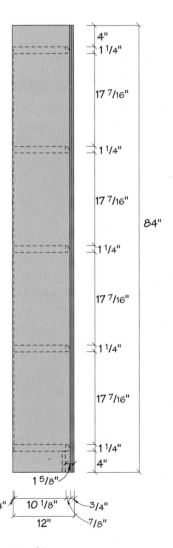

Profile

a practice joint because the depth of the groove is critical to a snug fit using this style of connector.

After cutting the slots in the shelves, lay out and mount the small part of the tapered connector to the side. The large connector will mount to the shelf groove with the wide end toward the shelf front. Do a test fit on the shelves. The shelves in the side units should be flush to the rabbet in the back edge of the sides. The center shelves should be flush with the back.

The next step is to cut the stopped grooves in the rest of the shelves for the hidden wire shelf supports. If your blade is too narrow, take two cuts to get the ¹⁄₈" groove necessary to slide the shelf onto the wire supports. Some drill and chisel work will be necessary to lengthen the kerf to accept the entire 9³⁄₄" length of the shelf wire. This requires drilling and chiseling into the end of the front edge. Lay out and drill the locations for the wire supports in the side and center sections so the shelf heights will match across the bookcase.

Now it's time for all the parts to come together. Begin by assembling the two outside units of the bookcase. Tip them onto their backs and attach the aprons to the bottom shelf using cleats and screws. Next attach the side units together forming the center section. The best way to do this is to assemble with the front facing up. Use a hand screw clamp to hold the sides while you're assembling. The apron on the center bottom can be screwed onto the shelf and braced with corner blocks prior to assembly. Push the lower shelf into place and mark the location of the apron, also called a kick or a base. Then remove the shelf and add two stop blocks to the sides to support the center apron from behind.

When you're happy with the fit of the parts, disassemble the bookcase and finish. I applied a coat of light stain to give the maple an aged appearance. (I used about two ounces of linseed oil and colored it with Olympic stains, one-half Early American No. 41552, and one-half Red Oak No. 41567, using ¹⁄₄ teaspoon of each.) Wipe on an even coat of oil. Wipe off the excess and let it dry for 24 hours. The next day, lightly sand the surfaces and clean them with a tack rag. Finish with two or three coats of a clear finish. ∎

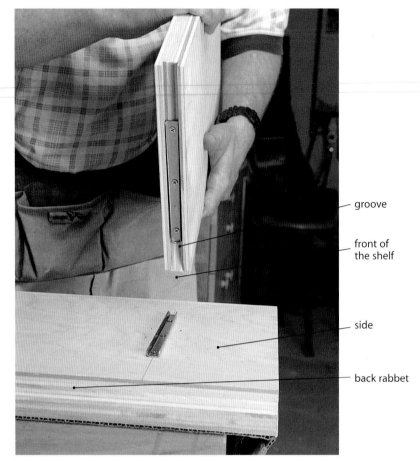

groove

front of the shelf

side

back rabbet

3 Use a dado stack to cut a ³⁄₄" x ³⁄₈" groove in the shelf's edge for the "magic wire" hardware. The groove should run from the point at which the solid wood edging meets the plywood shelf to the back of the shelf. The knockdown hardware is mounted in about the middle of the shelf. It pulls together pretty tightly, so you might want to sand any bumps or ridges off the ends of the shelves to keep from scratching the sides.

shelf wire

4 After cutting the ¹⁄₈" grooves in the shelf sides, assemble the case. Tap the wire shelf supports in and slide the loose shelves in place.

desktop pencil
BOX

Tired of losing your prized Mont Blanc in the black hole that is your lap drawer? Use one piece of wood and flocking to line the inside to create a handsome desktop box for your prized writing instruments.

I AM A CERTIFIABLE PEN-COLLECTING NUT. When I was younger, my mom worked in a doctor's office and would get pens from the salesmen that came to her office. I never quite got over getting those cheesy pens that looked like hipbones and surgical replacement parts. Now, my tastes run toward more classic writing instruments. This box is a great way to store my prized pens and mechanical pencils.

Choose Wood and Cut Out the Box

The box starts out as one slab of canary wood. This wood is highly figured, and you have to choose your stock carefully to avoid making a box that will blow apart on you. A piece roughly $1\frac{5}{8}" \times 3\frac{1}{2}" \times 13\frac{1}{4}"$ will yield a lid and box.

Begin by band sawing the lid from the slab. The lid might warp when you cut it as tension is released in the wood, so leave a little extra thickness for restraightening. Plane the larger part of the slab to $1\frac{1}{8}"$ thick. Affix the full-size pattern at right to the wood. This is the best time to mortise the piano hinge. Fold the hinge back on itself and place it, centered, on the back edge of the box. Draw an outline of the hinge and rout a mortise that is a little less than half the thickness of the hinge when closed. Place the lid on the box and transfer the ends of the mortise to the lid. Repeat the mortising process. Cut out the ellipses on the ends of the box and sand smooth. Mount the lid to the box. Turn the box over and cut the ellipses on the lid. Sand it flush with the box, and remove the lid.

Work the Inside

Drill holes on what will be the inside of the box. Cut out the inside using a scroll saw. Sand the inside of the box using a spindle sander. At this point, rout a $\frac{1}{8}" \times \frac{1}{8}"$ rabbet in the bottom edge of the box. It is better to do this on a router table than holding the router.

Rip a piece of Baltic birch for the bottom that is the correct width for the rabbet but is a little long. Place it over the box's rabbet and draw the outline of the ellipse. Band saw out the bottom and fit it into the rabbet. Glue the bottom in place with wood glue. Use masking tape to hold it until dry. Fit two $\frac{1}{4}"$-thick dividers in place inside the box. Use the lines left from the glued-down pattern as a guide. Glue them in place.

Shape the Lid

Begin shaping the lid by cutting the profile on the top as shown in the diagram. Use a plane and sandpaper to shape the profile. It's arbitrary as to when you're finished with the profile. Just make sure that the transition from the front angle to the end ellipses is smooth. As a finishing touch, use

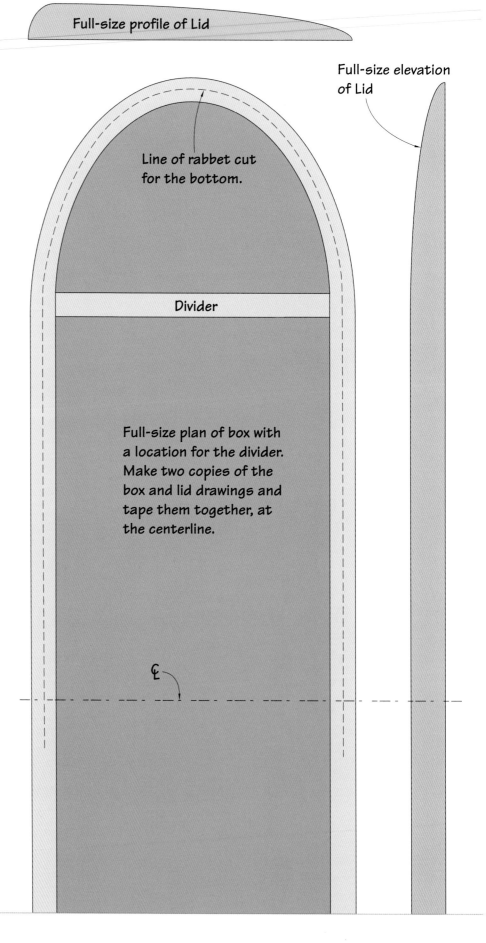

Full-size profile of Lid

Full-size elevation of Lid

Line of rabbet cut for the bottom.

Divider

Full-size plan of box with a location for the divider. Make two copies of the box and lid drawings and tape them together, at the centerline.

supplies

Lee Valley, www.leevalley.com, (800) 871-8158

- Hinge, item# 00D50.09, $3.70
- No. 0 screws, item# 91Z00.01, $2.40 box of 100
- Flocking gun, item# 98k10.02, $4.95
- Black flocking, item# 98K08.33, $6.95
- Black adhesive, item# 98K06.53, $6.95

a rotary tool to grind a small notch in the underside of the lid front for a finger pull. After finish sanding, spray three coats of laquer on all surfaces. It's important to seal the inside of the box. This will give the flocking adhesive a smooth surface to stick to.

Add the Lining

Follow the instructions on the flocking kit and line the inside of the box. Try a sample piece before tackling the box. Make sure to put masking tape on the top edge of the box so you will have a sharp transition from liner to wood.

After drying overnight, assemble the lid and box. When it's all said and done, it may take you longer to find your good pens in that lap drawer than it took to make this box. ■

cutting list **(inches):** *desktop pencil box*

No.	Item	Dimensions T W L	Material
1	Lid	³⁄₈" x 3¹⁄₂" x 13"	Canary wood
1	Box	1¹⁄₈" x 3¹⁄₂" x 13"	Canary wood
1	Bottom	¹⁄₄" x 3¹⁄₄" x 12³⁄₄"	Plywood
2	Dividers	¹⁄₄" x ⁷⁄₈" x 3"	Plywood

cutting list **(millimeters):** *desktop pencil box*

No.	Item	Dimensions T W L	Material
1	Lid	10 x 89 x 330	Canary wood
1	Box	29 x 89 x 330	Canary wood
1	Bottom	6 x 82 x 324	Plywood
2	Dividers	6 x 22 x 76	Plywood

guest room
MURPHY BED

Don't waste space in your guest room. Use it as an office or den when company leaves.

MY MOTHER-IN-LAW VISITS ABOUT TWICE A year. I happen to like her, so it was out of the question to make her sleep on a lumpy hide-a-bed. But I also didn't want to give up an entire room in my house to twice-a-year use. To compromise I opted for an idea born in the early 1900s — the Murphy bed. It's a handy guest bed when needed, but the bed can fold into the wall and give your house a bonus room.

The design of this piece is best described as "classic contemporary." To me it just looks nice. Probably the trickiest step is the columns. I'm not a fan of the lathe (great tool, I just don't like to use it), and I went out of my way to build the columns without turning a thing. I'll show you how later.

The rest of the project is simple case construction. The "magic" of the bed is store-bought. There are a number of Murphy bed mechanism kits available, but I prefer the piston operation of this unit. Though it's expensive at $185, the kit includes a comprehensive set of instructions for building the center bed section of the unit.

Buy a Bed Kit

Construction begins with the purchase and review of the bed mechanism kit. This center section determines the height and depth of the side cabinets. Once your dimensions are set, head to the saw. You'll need about five sheets of $\frac{3}{4}$" plywood (two sides good), and two sheets of $\frac{1}{4}$" plywood (which seems impossible to find two sides good, but if you can, great). Choose the best pieces for the bed panel and the outside ends of the unit. Cut the panels to the sizes given in the cutting list, then go get your iron.

This piece uses a lot of iron-on veneer tape. The other option was solid wood edging, which is a lot more work.

1 The foot end of the bed section shows the corner braces as well as the foot and locking hardware provided in the Murphy bed mechanism kit. When the feet are closed, the rods extend up into holes drilled in the cabinet top to hold the bed in place while stowed away.

No Lathes For Me!

There is turning involved in the columns, and it was done by Midwest Dowel Works, (800) 555-0133, who sold me 2" x 4' poplar dowels (item# LD-2000) for $18.13 each. The rest took some thinking, a table saw, a band saw, a router table and some sanding. A disc sander is handy, but you can do without it. The four column caps come from a piece of $1\frac{1}{2}$"-thick maple. Cut blocks $3\frac{1}{2}$" x $3\frac{1}{2}$", then mark a point centered from left-to-right and $1\frac{1}{2}$" from one edge. Mark this edge as your reference edge. Drill a hole at the intersection, then make a simple circle jig by driving a nail into a board $1\frac{1}{4}$" from one edge. Clip off the nail head. By clamping the board to the band saw with the nail $1\frac{1}{2}$" from the $\frac{1}{8}$" blade (leave a little extra room for sanding) you can turn fairly accurate circles. Repeat this step in $\frac{3}{4}$"-thick maple for the eight column-base spacers. By using a $\frac{3}{8}$" roundover bit chucked into my router table, I was able to turn a decent bead on the edges of the spacers. I then switched to a cove bit and ran a nice lifting detail to the underside of the caps. The octagonal pedestals were actually the easiest step. Starting with a 3" x 3" x 6" maple block, I set my table saw to a 45° angle and set the blade to cut a $\frac{13}{16}$" chamfer face. By rotating each block four times, the octagonal pedestal formed quickly. After careful sanding (there were a couple of burn marks) I nailed the base spacers to the pedestals, then doweled the larger 2" dowels between the base assembly and the cap.

step 1 One of the base spacers is marked and drilled for circle-cutting. The jig is clamped in place on the band saw.

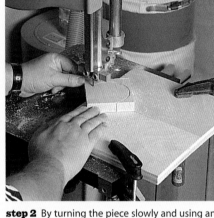

step 2 By turning the piece slowly and using an appropriately thin blade, which is tensioned correctly, fairly consistent circles can be achieved.

step 3 Using the same jig clamped to a combinations belt/disc sander, the band saw blade marks can be removed easily and the discs made even more uniform.

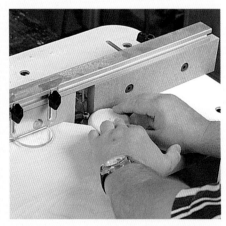

step 4 Using bearing-mounted bits and a clipped stop block clamped to the table, the spacers and caps can be shaped by slowly rotating the piece (counterclockwise) against the bit. Start slowly and increase the pressure as the cut deepens. I've moved the guard out of the way for the photo, but it should be right over the workpiece with $\frac{1}{16}$" to spare.

Make the Bed Frame

First, cut and assemble the seven L braces and side frame rails that support the mattress. The location of one of the braces is critical to the hardware for the legs.

Next, apply veneer tape to the four edges of the face panel, to the top edge and ends of the head rail and foot rail, and to the top edge of the two bed side rails and the headboard. While you're ironing, veneer the front edge of the two cabinet sides as well, then cut out the cabinet top and attach the top front and rear rails as shown in the diagram.

On this unit the poplar frame is screwed to the two bed side rails, then the frame is attached between the head and foot rails using a corner brace at the foot rail and screws through the head rail at the other end. Then lay the frame on the face panel and screw it in place through the braces.

2 The face frame is glued to the front of the lower cabinets. The back is tacked in place to hold the cabinet square.

— mounting strips

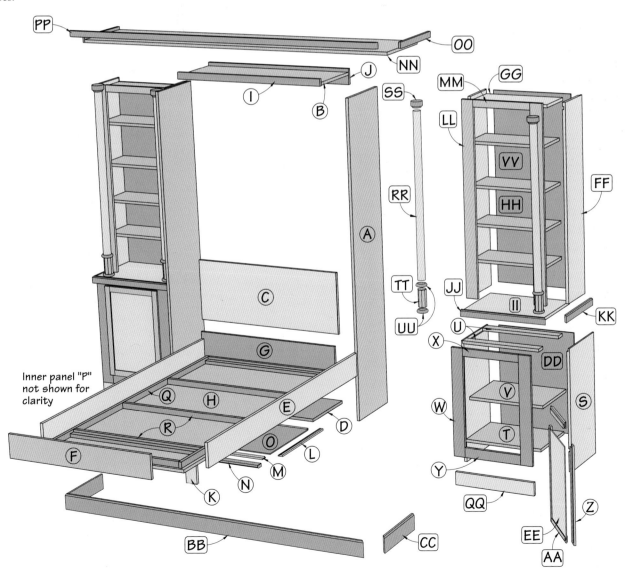

Inner panel "P" not shown for clarity

cutting list (**inches**): *murphy bed*

BED CENTER SECTION

No.	Ltr.	Item	Dimensions T W L	Material
2	A	Cabinet sides	$^3/_4$" x 16" x 81$^5/_{16}$"	CP
1	B	Cabinet top	$^3/_4$" x 14$^1/_2$" x 41$^3/_8$"	CP
1	C	Headboard	$^3/_4$" x 14$^1/_2$" x 41$^3/_8$"	CP
1	D	Bottom	$^3/_4$" x 16" x 41$^3/_8$"	P
2	E	Bed side rails	$^3/_4$" x 6" x 75"	CP
1	F	Foot rail	$^3/_4$" x 6" x 40$^1/_2$"	CP
1	G	Head rail	$^3/_4$" x 7$^7/_8$" x 40$^1/_2$"	CP
1	H	Face panel	$^3/_4$" x 41" x 76$^3/_4$"	CP
1	I	Top front rail	$^3/_4$" x 1$^3/_4$" x 41$^3/_8$"	C
1	J	Top rear rail	$^3/_4$" x 4" x 41$^3/_8$"	C
2	K	Legs	$^3/_4$" x 3" x 7"	C
4	L	Door stiles	$^1/_2$" x 1$^1/_2$" x 24"	C
4	M	Door rails	$^1/_2$" x 1$^1/_2$" x 14$^1/_8$"	C
1	N	Chair rail	$^3/_4$" x 1$^3/_4$" x 41"	C
2	O	Door panels	$^1/_4$" x 14$^3/_{16}$" x 21$^{15}/_{16}$"	CP
1	P	Inner panel	$^1/_4$" x 38$^7/_8$" x 74$^7/_8$"	P
2	Q	Frame side rails	$^7/_8$" x 1$^1/_2$" x 75"	PP
10	R	'L' frame braces	$^7/_8$" x 1$^1/_2$" x 37$^1/_2$"	PP

LOWER CABINETS

No.	Ltr.	Item	Dimensions T W L	Material
4	S	Sides	$^3/_4$" x 15$^1/_4$" x 31$^1/_4$"	CP
2	T	Bottoms	$^3/_4$" x 14$^1/_2$" x 21$^1/_4$"	CP
4	U	Mounting strips	$^3/_4$" x 2$^1/_2$" x 21$^1/_4$"	P
2	V	Shelves	$^3/_4$" x 14$^3/_8$" x 20$^3/_8$"	CP
4	W	Face frame stiles	$^3/_4$" x 3$^1/_4$" x 27$^7/_8$"	C
2	X	Upper face rails	$^3/_4$" x 1$^7/_8$" x 15$^3/_8$"	C
2	Y	Lower face rails	$^3/_4$" x 2" x 15$^3/_8$"	C
4	Z	Door stiles	$^3/_4$" x 1$^1/_2$" x 24"	C
4	AA	Door rails	$^3/_4$" x 1$^1/_2$" x 14$^1/_8$"	C
1	BB	Base front	$^3/_4$" x 4" x 88$^1/_4$"	C
2	CC	Base sides	$^3/_4$" x 4" x 16$^3/_4$"	C
2	DD	Backs	$^1/_4$" x 21$^5/_{16}$" x 26$^1/_2$"	CP
2	EE	Door panels	$^1/_4$" x 14$^3/_{16}$" x 21$^{15}/_{16}$"	CP

UPPER CABINETS

No.	Ltr.	Item	Dimensions T W L	Material
4	FF	Sides	$^3/_4$" x 10$^1/_4$" x 49$^1/_4$"	CP
2	GG	Tops	$^3/_4$" x 9$^1/_2$" x 21$^1/_4$"	CP
8	HH	Shelves	$^3/_4$" x 9$^3/_8$" x 20$^3/_8$"	CP
2	II	Countertops	$^3/_4$" x 16" x 22$^1/_8$"	CP
2	JJ	Counter edging	$^3/_4$" x 1$^3/_4$" x 23$^5/_8$"	C
2	KK	Counter edging	$^3/_4$" x 1$^3/_4$" x 16$^3/_4$"	C
4	LL	Face frame	$^3/_4$" x 3$^1/_2$" x 49$^1/_4$"	C
2	MM	Face frame	$^3/_4$" x 1$^3/_4$" x 15$^7/_{16}$"	C
1	NN	Cap piece	$^3/_4$" x 16$^3/_4$" x 88$^1/_4$"	P
2	OO	Cap side edging	$^3/_4$" x 1$^1/_2$" x 16$^3/_4$"	PP
1	PP	Cap front edging	$^3/_4$" x 1$^1/_2$" x 89$^3/_4$"	PP
2	QQ	Base spacers	$^3/_4$" x 3$^1/_4$" x 21$^3/_4$"	CP
4	RR	Columns	2" x 41$^3/_4$" dowels	PP
4	SS	Column caps	1$^1/_2$" x 3" discs	M
4	TT	Column pedestals	3" x 4$^3/_8$" octagons	M
8	UU	Column spacers	$^3/_4$" x 3" discs	M
2	VV	Backs	$^1/_4$" x 21$^5/_{16}$" x 48$^5/_8$"	CP

100 linear feet of $^7/_8$" cherry veneer tape
CP= Cherry plywood • C = Solid cherry • P = Birch plywood
M = Maple • PP=Poplar

---

cutting list (**millimeters**): *murphy bed*

BED CENTER SECTION

No.	Ltr.	Item	Dimensions T W L	Material
2	A	Cabinet sides	19 x 406 x 2065	CP
1	B	Cabinet top	19 x 369 x 1051	CP
1	C	Headboard	19 x 369 x 1051	CP
1	D	Bottom	19 x 406 x 1051	P
2	E	Bed side rails	19 x 152 x 1905	CP
1	F	Foot rail	19 x 152 x 1029	CP
1	G	Head rail	19 x 200 x 1029	CP
1	H	Face panel	19 x 1041 x 1949	CP
1	I	Top front rail	19 x 45 x 1051	C
1	J	Top rear rail	19 x 102 x 1051	C
2	K	Legs	19 x 76 x 178	C
4	L	Door stiles	13 x 38 x 610	C
4	M	Door rails	13 x 38 x 459	C
1	N	Chair rail	19 x 45 x 1041	C
2	O	Door panels	6 x 361 x 357	CP
1	P	Inner panel	6 x 987 x 1902	P
2	Q	Frame side rails	22 x 38 x 1905	PP
10	R	'L' frame braces	22 x 38 x 953	PP

LOWER CABINETS

No.	Ltr.	Item	Dimensions T W L	Material
4	S	Sides	19 x 387 x 793	CP
2	T	Bottoms	19 x 369 x 539	CP
4	U	Mounting strips	19 x 318 x 539	P
2	V	Shelves	19 x 366 x 518	CP
4	W	Face frame stiles	19 x 82 x 708	C
2	X	Upper face rails	19 x 47 x 391	C
2	Y	Lower face rails	19 x 51 x 391	C
4	Z	Door stiles	19 x 38 x 610	C
4	AA	Door rails	19 x 38 x 359	C
1	BB	Base front	19 x 102 x 2241	C
2	CC	Base sides	19 x 102 x 425	C
2	DD	Backs	6 x 541 x 673	CP
2	EE	Door panels	6 x 361 x 587	CP

UPPER CABINETS

No.	Ltr.	Item	Dimensions T W L	Material
4	FF	Sides	19 x 260 x 1251	CP
2	GG	Tops	19 x 242 x 539	CP
8	HH	Shelves	19 x 239 x 518	CP
2	II	Countertops	19 x 406 x 562	CP
2	JJ	Counter edging	19 x 45 x 600	C
2	KK	Counter edging	19 x 45 x 425	C
4	LL	Face frame	19 x 89 x 1251	C
2	MM	Face frame	19 x 45 x 392	C
1	NN	Cap piece	19 x 425 x 2241	P
2	OO	Cap side edging	19 x 38 x 425	PP
1	PP	Cap front edging	19 x 38 x 2230	PP
2	QQ	Base spacers	19 x 82 x 552	CP
4	RR	Columns	51 x 1060 dowels	PP
4	SS	Column caps	35 x 76 discs	M
4	TT	Column pedestals	76 x 112 octagons	M
8	UU	Column spacers	19 x 76 discs	M
2	VV	Backs	6 x 541 x 1235	CP

30.5 linear meters of 22mm cherry veneer tape
CP= Cherry plywood • C = Solid cherry • P = Birch plywood
M = Maple • PP=Poplar

Build the Bed Cabinet and Mount the Bed Frame

Now you're ready to assemble the bed cabinet. Follow the hardware instructions provided by the manufacturer for accurate placement of the braces and hinges.

To mount the bed frame in the cabinet, first attach the cabinet top between the two sides, then slide the bed section between the sides, spreading the sides to allow the pivot hinges to slip into place. Screw the bottom and headboard in place between the sides. Don't worry about the screws through the sides showing because the side cabinets will cover all of them except at the cabinet top, which will be visible for the front 6".

Make the Cabinets

With the center section complete, the rest is face frame cabinetry. Similar joinery is used on both upper and lower cabinets, so cut out the pieces at the same time. The cabinet backs fit into $\frac{1}{2}$" × $\frac{3}{8}$"-wide rabbets cut on the back of the upper and lower sides. Also cut a $\frac{3}{4}$" × $\frac{3}{8}$" rabbet on the top edge of each lower side to attach the mounting strips.

Next, set up to run $\frac{3}{8}$" × $\frac{3}{4}$"-wide grooves for the tops in the upper cabinets and for the bottoms in the lower cabinets. The top grooves are located 1" down from the top of the sides; the lower cabinet grooves are 4$\frac{3}{4}$" up from the floor.

When assembling the side cabinets, use screws through the inner sides into the top and bottom pieces, and glue and clamp the outer sides. Make sure to hold the tops and bottoms flush to the inside of the back rabbets. Use the backs to square the cabinets during assembly, tacking them in place with some brads that can be removed for finishing.

While the glue is drying, cut the two countertops and the solid wood edging for the front and outer side. Cut a $\frac{1}{2}$" × $\frac{3}{8}$" stopped rabbet on the back edge of each top to allow the upper cabinet back to attach to the tops. The front edging on each top is left $\frac{3}{4}$" long on the inside corner to allow the edging to lip over the cabinet sides of the center section. Cut a 45° chamfer on the tops to form a $\frac{5}{8}$" chamfer face, then miter the joint and glue the edging in place.

extended edging

3 The completed countertops are attached to the assembled upper cabinets by screwing through the sides and into the face frame. Note the solid edging on the top that extends past the top to cover the center cabinet side.

4 The assembled upper cabinet is secured to the lower cabinet by screwing up through the mounting strips into the countertops.

Build the Face Frames

Next biscuit the face frames together and glue them to the upper and lower cabinets. The frames should flush up against the top surface in the upper cabinets and on the bottoms in the lower cabinets.

When the clamps are off, finish sand the cabinets and countertops. Attach the tops to the upper cabinets, screwing through the tops into the upper sides. Then attach the upper cabinets to the lower cabinets by screwing through the mounting strips.

Now put the side cabinets in place on either side of the center cabinet and attach them with 1¼" screws through the outer cabinet's inner sides. Hide the screws behind the face frame.

Make and Attach the Doors

There are four doors for this unit, but only two function. The doors in the side cabinets are lipped doors, so only ½" of the frame extends beyond the cabinet front. To continue the facade of four actual doors, the two center doors are ½" thick and nailed to the face panel.

I used stub tenons and grooves for the doors, allowing the ¼" panels to float in the groove used for the tenons. The same tenon-and-groove setup can be used on the ½" and ¾" door frame pieces as long as the setups start from the outer face of each door, so the groove on the ½" doors becomes a rabbet.

To attach the center doors to the face panel, approach it as a moulding project and mount the doors in pieces as shown above in photo 5.

Assemble the outer doors and mount them to the cabinets. I used European hardware to hide the hinges and added mounting blocks for the hinges to the back of the face frame. I also had to add a ¼" × ½" strip to the inside of the door to support the hinge specified in the source box.

With the doors attached, cut, chamfer and attach the chair rail by screwing it from the inside of the face panel.

Create the Columns

Now build the columns and top cap. The cap is a piece of plywood with poplar edging nailed to the front and side edges. Round corners at a 1½" radius to soften the look, then sand and paint the piece

5 The false doors attach quickly using a brad nailer. The spacing should be even across the face panel.

black. The columns are explained in detail in "No Lathes For Me!" on page 64.

The 4" base across the front of the cabinets and on the sides of the outer cabinets has the same chamfer cut on the top edge as the countertops. Add spacer blocks to the front of the lower cabinets below the face frame to support the base pieces. The base should be fit and attached after finishing and installing the cabinets to provide the best fit and to tie the cabinets together visually. Finally, cut some shelves and find the veneer tape again. I made adjustable shelves, drilling five holes per shelf at 1" intervals.

I knew with this large a piece I didn't want a dark cherry finish. I was so pleased with this finish I want to pass it along to you. I used Pratt & Lambert's Tonetic's Eastern Red Cedar stain. It gives an even finish that makes the wood look aged but doesn't cover the intricacies of the grain. A couple of coats of a satin finish lacquer and the unit is ready to install.

The room works great as a reading room and could easily become an office. But when Mom stops by, she knows she'll be comfortable. ∎

supplies

Rockler, www.rockler.com, (800) 279-4441
• 1 - halogen light set, item# 44264, $69.99

Woodcraft, www.woodcraft.com (800) 225-1153
• 2 - bags of ¼" shelf pins, item# 27i11, $1.99 each
• 1 - Murphy twin bed mechanism, item# 130708, $184.99

Woodworker's Supply, (800) 645-9292
• 2 - pair hinges, item# 937-086, $4.50/pair

Spokane Hardware Supply www.spokane-hardware.com (800) 708-6649
• 2 - handles, item# DP40-BL, $5.46 each

Midwest Dowel Works, (800) 555-0133
• 4 - poplar dowels, 2" x 4'

great danish

modern table

DON'T HATE ME BECAUSE I FOUND SOME 20"-wide curly maple. It was a lucky accident, and while it wasn't cheap ($50), it was a good deal. The only way to show off this 20" × 60" piece was as a tabletop, and I'd been itching to try something Danish.

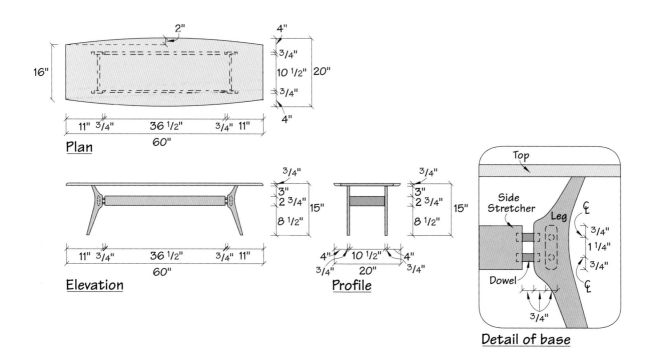

Plan

Elevation

Profile

Detail of base
Top
Side Stretcher
Leg
Dowel

cutting list **(inches):** *great danish modern table*

No.	Item	Dimensions T W L	Material
4	Legs	$3/4$" x 5" x $14^1/4$"	Walnut
2	Side stretchers	$3/4$" x $2^3/4$" x $36^1/2$"	Walnut
2	End stretchers	$3/4$" x $2^3/4$" x $10^1/2$"	Walnut
16	Dowels	$3/8$"x $1^1/2$"	Maple
1	Top	$3/4$" x 20" x 60"	Maple

cutting list **(millimeters):** *great danish modern table*

No.	Item	Dimensions T W L	Material
4	Legs	19 x 127 x 362	Walnut
2	Side stretchers	19 x 70 x 927	Walnut
2	End stretchers	19 x 70 x 267	Walnut
16	Dowels	10 x 38	Maple
1	Top	19 x 508 x 1524	Maple

Mill the Wood

First, mill all your material to $3/4$" thickness. The schedule includes four blanks for the legs that will yield one leg per piece. If you're being thrifty, the pieces will interlock and save material, but orient the grain so it follows the path of the lower part of the leg. Use the pattern on page 71 to lay out the legs.

Cut the Legs

Use a band saw or jigsaw to cut the legs to shape. Use double-sided tape to hold the four legs together. Sand the edges of all four legs at the same time.

Soften all the edges (except the ends of the end stretchers and the tops and bottoms of the legs) using a $1/4$" roundover bit. Then mark the dowel locations as shown in the diagrams and drill the holes.

Sand the Project

Sand the entire base through 220 grit, then glue the legs to the side stretchers, seating the dowels in the holes to leave $3/4$" of the dowel exposed. Then glue the end stretchers between the two side pieces.

Lay Out and Finish the Top

Now lay out the top. Bend a strip of $1/4$" material along the edges of the top to mark the gentle curve, then cut the top to shape. For an interesting effect, I routed the edges of the top with a $1/2$" roundover. I cut this detail on the bottom of the sides and the top of the ends. I then marked a line 1" in from the edges and used a random-orbit sander to further roll the edge details toward the 1" line.

I finished the table with natural Danish oil, then fastened the top to the legs using figure-eight table fasteners placed parallel to the side stretchers. This way the fasteners will move if the top piece moves. ∎

supplies

Woodcraft, www.woodcraft.com
(800) 225-1153

• Top fasteners, item# 130216, $3.50/10

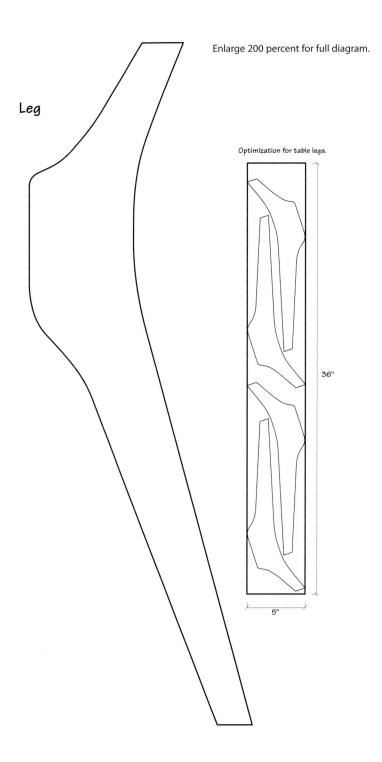

Leg

Enlarge 200 percent for full diagram.

Optimization for table legs.

36"

5"

A Danish Oil Finish That Is Awesome

Danish oil is more than just a name. It is a carefully blended finish that has been sometimes underused.

It can be applied with a paint brush, foam applicator or with a rag.

What I would like to suggest on this tabletop is an extra step that will give you a finish that will be the envy of all who see and feel it.

After you have finished sanding the tabletop, apply the Danish oil finish and let it soak into the wood for 5 to 10 minutes. Add more oil in the areas where it soaks into the wood and gets dry. After 10 minutes, wipe off all unabsorbed finish. Let this cure overnight.

The next day, pour some oil finish on the tabletop and start wetsanding using 600 grit wet/dry sandpaper and a flat sanding block. Apply more oil as needed to keep the sandpaper lubricated.

You will begin to see a slurry form as you're sanding. This slurry will start filling the minute pores in the wood. Keep sanding until you see a satiny sheen begin to develop. Sand the entire tabletop. Wipe off all excess slurry and oil, and let this cure overnight.

In the morning, you should see a very smooth and polished finish. If you desire a more glossy finish, repeat the above sanding procee-dure until the desired sheen is reached.

modern
wardrobe

Use subtle black accents to complement the understated grain pattern on this maple chest.

FURNITURE DESIGN IN THE LAST TWO centuries has swung back and forth wildly between austere and outrageous. One year everything's rococo and carved; the next year the far simpler Hepplewhite style is the thing. Then comes the ornate Victorian stuff, followed immediately by the straight-lined Arts-and-Crafts style. It's no wonder furniture manufacturers stay in business.

If you haven't noticed yet, the United States is heading into another era where simple is better. And while some of these clean and contemporary pieces are criticized as merely boring wooden crates with drawers, others show off the elegant proportions of the furniture using only understated accents. We hope you'll agree the subtle black accents on this wardrobe have achieved that goal.

1 Before assembly it's best to mark and drill the locations for the shelf pins, and to lay out and mount the base plates for the hinges. As always, a little masking tape on the drill bit makes a handy depth stop.

European Hardware

European hardware is a broad term covering a number of hinges and shelving systems. Best known for its use in commercial furniture, I chose to use it in this piece for a number of reasons. The door hinges allow adjustment of the door in three dimensions after the door is attached, and it is invisible from the exterior of the piece, keeping the lines clean and simple. The hinges require a 35mm Forstner bit to drill holes for the hinges on the inside of the door, and a jig designed just for installing these hinges is available from Rockler, www.rockler.com, (800) 279-4441.

Contemporary decorative hardware can be tricky to find, so I was pleased to find Spokane Hardware on the Internet (see the Supplies box). Offering a large and varied selection of contemporary, fanciful and traditional hardware for sale on the Web, this site saves a lot of time running from store to store. The pulls selected for this piece are commercially available to cabinet shops, but it's nice to find them accessible for the home woodworker as well.

This was the first time I'd used the drawer front adjusters, though they've been available for years. Having fought with adjusting drawer fronts on inset and flush-mount drawers forever, I found these clever plastic devices to be a big help. Allowing 1/8" adjustment in any direction, fine-tuning a drawer front is now a snap rather than a chore. Though the instructions specify a 25mm bit to mount the adjuster in the drawer face, a 1" Forstner works admirably with a little shimming.

THE WARDROBE USES FRAMELESS construction, and it is built almost entirely of plywood so it's stable and lightweight. The visible plywood edges are covered with iron-on veneer tape to retain the simple, clean lines of the piece. The concealed hinges provide smooth door operation without interrupting the proportions of the door and drawer arrangement of the front. The pulls are unobtrusive and echo the black line of the reveal at the top, bottom and black base.

Cut Out the Parts

Construction begins by cutting the case pieces to size. Next, cut 3/8" × 3/4" rabbets on the back, top and bottom of both side pieces to accept the back, top and bottom. Also rabbet the top and bottom pieces on the back edge to hold the back. Now cut a 3/8"-deep by 3/4"-wide dado in the top and bottom pieces to leave an 11" opening between the right side and the vertical partition.

Before rushing to assemble the case, there are a few things to do first. Cut your four drawer dividers to size and apply veneer tape to the front edge of each. Mark the locations of the drawer dividers and decide whether you want to use biscuits or dowels to hold the drawer dividers in place between the left side and the partition. The drawer openings are graduated in size and should be as follows from top to bottom: 5", 5 7/8", 7 1/4", 9" and 11 1/8".

Because the door section of the wardrobe is only 11" wide, it's a good idea to predrill the right side and partition for shelf pins and also for the European-style hinge plates before assembly. One more preassembly task: Sand the inside of the shelf section and the part of the back that's visible. You'll be glad you did.

Assemble the Case

Now assemble the case using glue and by driving nails through the top and bottom pieces into the sides and partition. When in place, the drawer dividers should be proud of the front edge of the case by the thickness of the veneer tape. Lastly, nail the back in place into the rabbets. This will square up the case.

With the case assembled, go nab your spouse's iron. Apply veneer tape to the front edges of the case and to the top of

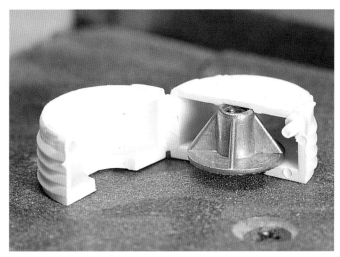

2 The drawer face adjuster is a simple plastic pocket with a metal nut captured inside. When attached, the nut will slide freely within the plastic case, allowing the face to be moved $1/8$" in any direction.

4 I cut the top and back recesses for the handles using the same jig. Unfortunately I made my jig a little short and had to move the clamps between cuts. Make your jig the width of the drawer and to fit your own router template guides, and you'll be in good shape.

3 The hardboard reveal strip is painted black, then mitered to extend beyond the front of the cabinet itself. The reveal strip is recessed $1/4$" in from the edges of the top.

wood words

REVEAL: A decorative detail formed by offsetting a portion of the side to form a recessed feature. This can be done by adding pieces, or a groove can be cut in the material to create the same effect.

PROUD: Where two pieces meet with one slightly raised above the other, it is said to be "proud."

the case on the front edge and sides to hide the rabbet joint. The $7/8$"-wide tape is plenty because the reveal will only show $1/4$" of the top of the case.

The false top is simply a piece of plywood edged with veneer tape. Check the size against the finished size of the assembled case to make sure the false top's edges will be flush with the sides, front and back. The $1/4$" reveal between the top and case is created using strips of $1/4$" × 1" hardboard, with one edge spray painted black. Fit the strips to the underside of the top, allowing the $1/4$" setback on the front and sides. Add a fourth strip flush to the rear of the top to level it out. With the strips fit, use black enamel spray paint to coat the visible edge and the underside of the front piece, then attach the reveal strips to the underside of the top.

Now attach the false top to the case.

Drill clearance holes through the case and attach the false top using screws up through the inside of the case, again, flushing the back edges of the case and the false top.

The base is a simple frame held together by biscuits, dowels or mortise-and-tenon joinery, with the legs attached between the stretchers at the corners. With the base glued and assembled, add $\frac{1}{4}$" × $\frac{13}{16}$" hardboard strips to the top edge as you did to the underside of the top. Next, finish the base and strip with black paint to add visual "weight" at the base of the chest. When dry, attach the base to the cabinet using metal chair braces at the corners.

Make the Drawers

Now build the drawers using simple $\frac{1}{4}$" × $\frac{1}{2}$" rabbet joints on the sides, with the fronts and backs captured between the sides. The bottoms slide into $\frac{1}{4}$" × $\frac{1}{4}$" grooves in the sides and front that are cut $\frac{1}{2}$" up from the bottoms of the drawer pieces. The back is cut $\frac{1}{2}$" shorter than the front to allow the bottoms to slide into place. Use the bottoms to hold the drawers square while the glue dries, then remove them to make finishing the drawers easier. I set up a $\frac{1}{4}$" radius router bit in a router table and ran the top edges of the drawer parts (both sides) to make them more finger-friendly. Don't round over the front edge where the drawer face will attach. With the drawers assembled, attach the drawer slides to the cabinet and to the drawer sides and check for smooth operation.

Cover the edges of the drawer faces and the door with veneer tape. Then rout the shallow mortise centered in the top edge of each for the pulls. Use a router with a straight bit. Photo 4 shows the jig I built for doing this.

I want to mention that the screws provided with the pulls are roundhead screws. In an effort to keep things flush and simple, I used a countersink on the clearance holes in the pulls and then used flat-head screws to attach the pulls. Now attach the drawer faces to the drawers using the hardware shown in photo 2. This allows for easy adjustment of the drawer faces.

cutting list (inches): *modern wardrobe*

No.	Letter	Item	Dimensions T W L	Materials
2	A	Sides	$\frac{3}{4}$" x $17\frac{1}{4}$" x $42\frac{3}{4}$"	MP
1	B	Partition	$\frac{3}{4}$" x $16\frac{1}{2}$" x 42"	MP
2	C	Top & bottom	$\frac{3}{4}$" x $17\frac{1}{4}$" x $35\frac{1}{2}$"	MP
1	D	False Top	$\frac{3}{4}$" x 18" x 36"	MP
1	E	Back	$\frac{3}{4}$" x $35\frac{1}{4}$" x 42"	MP
1	F	Door	$\frac{3}{4}$" x 12" x $42\frac{1}{2}$"	MP
1	G	Drawer face	$\frac{3}{4}$" x 12" x $23\frac{7}{8}$"	MP
1	H	Drawer face	$\frac{3}{4}$" x $9\frac{9}{16}$" x $23\frac{7}{8}$"	MP
1	I	Drawer face	$\frac{3}{4}$" x $7\frac{13}{16}$" x $23\frac{7}{8}$"	MP
1	J	Drawer face	$\frac{3}{4}$" x $6\frac{7}{16}$" x $23\frac{7}{8}$"	MP
1	K	Drawer face	$\frac{3}{4}$" x $5\frac{7}{8}$" x $23\frac{7}{8}$"	MP
4	L	Drawer dividers	$\frac{3}{4}$" x 2" x $22\frac{7}{8}$"	MP
3	M	Shelves	$\frac{3}{4}$" x 16" x $101\frac{5}{16}$"	MP
2	N	Drawer sides	$\frac{1}{2}$" x $10\frac{1}{16}$" x 16"	BB
2	O	Drawer sides	$\frac{1}{2}$" x $8\frac{1}{16}$" x 16"	BB
2	P	Drawer sides	$\frac{1}{2}$" x $6\frac{1}{4}$" x 16"	BB
2	Q	Drawer sides	$\frac{1}{2}$" x 5" x 16"	BB
2	R	Drawer sides	$\frac{1}{2}$" x 4" x 16"	BB
2	S	Drawer front & back	$\frac{1}{2}$" x $9\frac{9}{16}$" x $21\frac{1}{4}$"	BB
2	T	Drawer front & back	$\frac{1}{2}$" x $7\frac{9}{16}$" x $21\frac{1}{4}$"	BB
2	U	Drawer front & back	$\frac{1}{2}$" x $5\frac{3}{4}$" x $21\frac{1}{4}$"	BB
2	V	Drawer front & back	$\frac{1}{2}$" x $4\frac{1}{2}$" x $21\frac{1}{4}$"	BB
2	W	Drawer front & back	$\frac{1}{2}$" x $3\frac{1}{2}$" x $21\frac{1}{4}$"	BB
5	X	Drawer bottoms	$\frac{1}{4}$" x $21\frac{1}{4}$" x $15\frac{3}{4}$"	L
4	Y	Legs	$1\frac{1}{4}$" x $1\frac{1}{4}$" x 4"	P
2	Z	Base stretchers	$\frac{3}{4}$" x $1\frac{1}{4}$" x $33\frac{7}{16}$"	P
2	AA	Base stretchers	$\frac{3}{4}$" x $1\frac{1}{4}$" x $15\frac{9}{16}$"	P

9 - linear feet each of $\frac{1}{4}$" x 1" and $\frac{1}{4}$" x $\frac{13}{16}$" hardboard reveal strip
75 - linear feet of $\frac{7}{8}$" maple veneer tape
MP=Maple plywood   L= Luan plywood
BB=Baltic birch plywood   P=Poplar

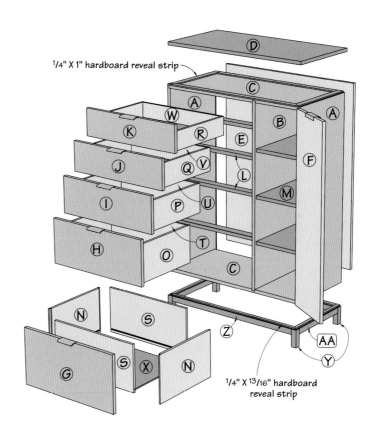

$\frac{1}{4}$" X 1" hardboard reveal strip

$\frac{1}{4}$" X $\frac{13}{16}$" hardboard reveal strip

cutting list (millimeters): *modern wardrobe*

No.	Letter	Item	Dimensions T W L	Materials
2	A	Sides	19 x 438 x 1086	MP
1	B	Partition	19 x 419 x 1067	MP
2	C	Top & bottom	19 x 438 x 902	MP
1	D	False Top	19 x 457 x 914	MP
1	E	Back	19 x 895 x 1067	MP
1	F	Door	19 x 305 x 1080	MP
1	G	Drawer face	19 x 305 x 606	MP
1	H	Drawer face	19 x 243 x 606	MP
1	I	Drawer face	19 x 199 x 606	MP
1	J	Drawer face	19 x 163 x 606	MP
1	K	Drawer face	19 x 149 x 606	MP
4	L	Drawer dividers	19 x 51 x 581	MP
3	M	Shelves	19 x 406 x 278	MP
2	N	Drawer sides	13 x 256 x 406	BB
2	O	Drawer sides	13 x 205 x 406	BB
2	P	Drawer sides	13 x 158 x 406	BB
2	Q	Drawer sides	13 x 127 x 406	BB
2	R	Drawer sides	13 x 102 x 406	BB
2	S	Drawer front & back	13 x 243 x 539	BB
2	T	Drawer front & back	13 x 192 x 539	BB
2	U	Drawer front & back	13 x 145 x 539	BB
2	V	Drawer front & back	13 x 114 x 539	BB
2	W	Drawer front & back	13 x 89 x 539	BB
5	X	Drawer bottoms	6 x 539 x 400	L
4	Y	Legs	32 x 32 x 102	P
2	Z	Base stretchers	19 x 32 x 849	P
2	AA	Base stretchers	19 x 32 x 395	P

2.75 - linear meters each of 6mm x 25mm and 6mm x 21mm hardboard reveal strip
23 - linear meters of 22mm maple veneer tape

MP=Maple plywood   L= Luan plywood
BB=Baltic birch plywood   P=Poplar

5 The drawer-face adjusters are attached by first drilling two clearance holes in the drawer box front. Then locate the approximate spacing of the drawer face on the drawer front (the closer the better), and make a mark through the clearance hole on the back of the face with a scratch awl. Remove the drawer box and drill the 1" holes for the adjusters. Then just screw the face on and adjust.

Attach the Hinges

Now drill the door to accept the European hinges and mount them to the cabinet. If you haven't used concealed hinges before, take a few minutes to play with the adjustment to get a feel for the versatility of these hinges.

Lastly, cut a groove the length of both sides of the shelves, and then add veneer tape to the front edge. The shelf pins slip into the slots in the shelves and provide invisible support. It's your choice whether to make the shelf locations adjustable by adding more shelf pin holes. I preferred to use set locations to keep the interior clean and unmarred.

Finish the Case

The case is now ready to finish. Remove the hardware and finish sanding the wardrobe. Use a clear finish everywhere, even over the black accent strips. After the finish has dried, attach the hardware and hang the door. Adjust the drawer fronts and door to make all the spaces equal. Then step back and enjoy the clean simple lines of your work — until the tastes of the furniture world swing back the other way. Then perhaps you'll have to apply some fancy moulding or something. ∎

supplies

Rockler, www.rockler.com, (800) 279-4441
- 5 Sets - 16" drawer slides, item# 161442, $4.99 each/set
- 1 Pair - hinges, item# 123032, $9.49 each
- 2 Packs - drawer face levelers, item# 110763, $5.99 each
- 1 Pack - shelf pins, item# 22286, $2.99 each

Spokane Hardware Supply
www.spokane-hardware.com
(800) 708-6649,
- 5 - handles, item# DP40-BL, $5.46 each

bauhaus
jewelry box

This project looks so much like a modern office building, you half expect to find tiny executives inside instead of jewelry.

IF THE FAMOUS BAUHAUS ARCHITECT Ludwig Mies van der Rohe (1886-1969) had designed a jewelry box, I imagine it would look a lot like one of his modern office buildings: starkly utilitarian and well-proportioned. This jewelry box was built with his design principles in mind. Instead of glass and steel, however, I chose to use figured wood — cherry in particular, with a curly cherry veneer top.

Big Box Made From Little Ones

The neat part of this jewelry box was not so much how it was made but what it was made from. I started with a single ½"-thick board about 11" × 60" for the sides. This ensures there will be a grain match on three corners of the box. The construction is simply a series of smaller boxes glued together to form one larger chest of drawers. The top is a curly cherry veneer and plywood panel glued into the top box.

Begin construction by planing down a single board to size, then rip the side widths of the individual layers, keeping track of their orientation. Next cut the profile on the bottom edge of each side blank as shown on the diagram, making the bevel cut first, then the rabbet. Use a rip blade to leave a square-bottomed cut in the rabbet.

Now you can separate each layer into the sides, front and back pieces. It takes four different setups to make all of the parts. These cuts can be made on a table saw or miter saw. Use one of the cutting lists on page 82 to organize the order of the cuts. When finished, the two outside ends of each original blank (which form the mismatched grain joint) will be at the back of the finished box. Mark the parts and their order.

Cut No. 3 (for mini-biscuits) biscuit slots in the two back corners of each layer. Tape the individual units together and take a general measurement of the dimensions inside the rabbet on each box. Now make the dividers that go between each drawer. I made these divider boxes by first building one box from a piece of cherry that was ¾" × 3½" × 55" and then ripping it into five 9⁄16" dividers. Make this large box with splined miter joints. Make sure the grain direction on the spline is the same as the grain direction on the box. Rip the five dividers from this box and fit them into the rabbets in the bottom of the drawer boxes.

Top It Off

Cut out the top according to the cutting list. Lay up a veneer sandwich with plywood, veneer, wax paper and backer panels for clamping (see photo 2). After the glue is dry, trim the excess veneer and glue a ¼" cherry strip to the front edge of the top.

When the panel is glued in place in the top box, the front corners of the panel

1 Cut the five dividers from one four-sided box. Tape all of the drawer boxes together and fit the dividers with a block plane.

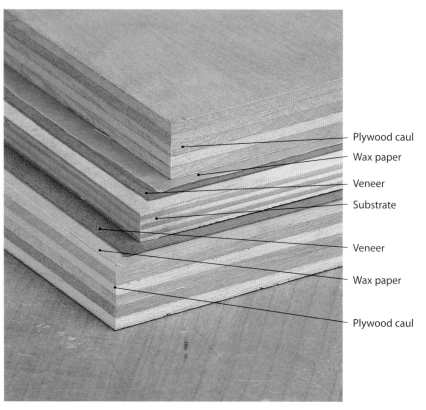

Plywood caul
Wax paper
Veneer
Substrate
Veneer
Wax paper
Plywood caul

2 From bottom to top, start with a plywood base plate, or caul, then wax paper to prevent adhesion to the plate. Then comes the veneer, and finally the substrate. In this case, Baltic birch. Repeat this order on the other side. Apply glue to the substrate and clamp it all up.

Scale diagram of cutting layout for case parts and dividers.
Scale: 1 1/2" = 1'-0"

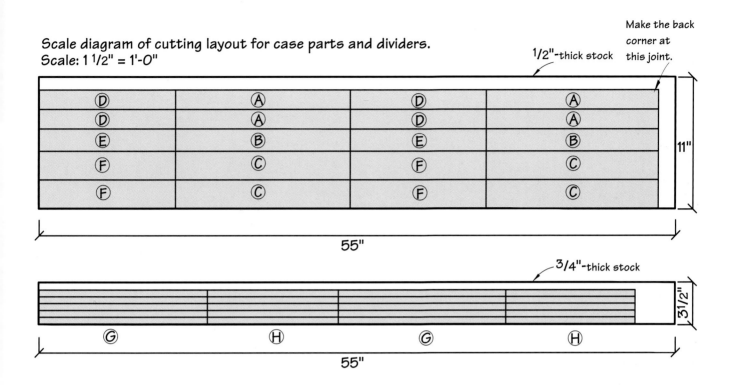

1/2"-thick stock

Make the back corner at this joint.

Ⓓ	Ⓐ	Ⓓ	Ⓐ
Ⓓ	Ⓐ	Ⓓ	Ⓐ
Ⓔ	Ⓑ	Ⓔ	Ⓑ
Ⓕ	Ⓒ	Ⓕ	Ⓒ
Ⓕ	Ⓒ	Ⓕ	Ⓒ

11"

55"

3/4"-thick stock

31/2"

Ⓖ   Ⓗ   Ⓖ   Ⓗ

55"

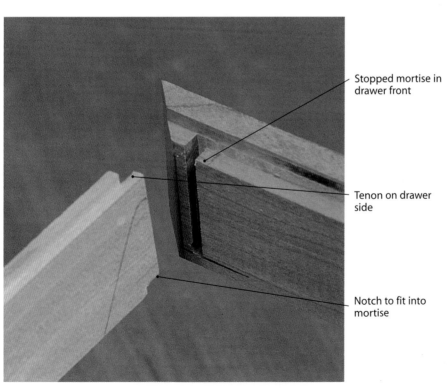

Stopped mortise in drawer front

Tenon on drawer side

Notch to fit into mortise

3 The drawers go together with a mortise and tenon. Lay out the mortise on the drawer front from the outside of where the drawer side will join the front. Mark 1/4" in from this mark. That's where the mortise will go. Mark the height of the tenon on the drawer front. Use a square as a guide and rout a 1/4"-deep mortise into the front. Rout a 1/8" x 1/4" rabbet into the inside bottom edge of the drawer front using a router mounted in a table.

cutting list (inches): *bauhaus jewelry box*

No.	Ltr.	Item	Dimensions T W L	Materials
4	A	Fronts & backs	$1/2$" x $1^5/8$" x 15"	Cherry
2	B	Fronts & backs	$1/2$" x $1^7/8$" x 15"	Cherry
4	C	Fronts & backs	$1/2$" x $2^3/8$" x 15"	Cherry
4	D	Ends	$1/2$" x $1^5/8$" x $11^3/4$"	Cherry
2	E	Ends	$1/2$" x $1^7/8$" x $11^3/4$"	Cherry
4	F	Ends	$1/2$" x $2^3/8$" x $11^3/4$"	Cherry
10	G	Case divdr f&b	$9/16$" x $3/4$" $14^1/2$"	Cherry
10	H	Case divdr ends	$9/16$" x $3/4$" x $11^1/4$"	Cherry
2	I	Drawer sides	$1/4$" x 1" x $10^{13}/16$"	Maple
1	J	Drawer back	$1/4$" x 1" x $13^{11}/16$"	Maple
2	K	Drawer sides	$1/4$" x $1^3/8$" x $10^{13}/16$"	Maple
1	L	Drawer back	$1/4$" x $1^3/8$" x $131^{11}/16$"	Maple
2	M	Drawer sides	$1/4$" x $1^5/8$" x $10^{13}/16$"	Maple
1	N	Drawer back	$1/4$" x $1^5/8$" x $13^{11}/16$"	Maple
4	O	Drawer sides	$1/4$" x $2^1/8$" x $10^{13}/16$"	Maple
2	P	Drawer backs	$1/4$" x $2^1/8$" x $13^{11}/16$"	Maple
5	Q	Drawer bottoms	$1/8$" x $10^{11}/16$" x $13^{11}/16$"	Masonite
7	R	Drawer dividers	$1/8$" x $1/2$" x $10^5/16$"	Maple
7	S	Drawer dividers	$1/8$" x $3/8$" x $13^7/16$"	Maple
7	T	Drawer dividers	$1/8$" x 1" x $10^5/16$"	Maple
5	U	Drawer dividers	$1/8$" x $5/8$" x $13^7/16$"	Maple
2	V	Drawer dividers	$1/8$" x $1^1/4$" x $10^5/16$"	Maple
2	W	Drawer dividers	$1/8$" x 1" x $13^7/16$"	Maple
4	X	Drawer dividers	$1/8$" x $1^1/2$" x $10^5/16$"	Maple
2	Y	Drawer dividers	$1/8$" x $1^1/4$" x $13^7/16$"	Maple
1	Z	Top	$3/8$" x $10^1/2$" x 14"	Maple
1	AA	Top trim	$1/4$" x $3/8$" x 14"	Maple

cutting list (millimeters): *bauhaus jewelry box*

No.	Letter	Item	Dimensions T W L	Materials
4	A	Fronts & backs	13 x 41 x 381	Cherry
2	B	Fronts & backs	13 x 47 x 381	Cherry
4	C	Fronts & backs	13 x 61 x 381	Cherry
4	D	Ends	13 x 41 x 298	Cherry
2	E	Ends	13 x 47 x 298	Cherry
4	F	Ends	13 x 61 x 298	Cherry
10	G	Case divdr f&b	14 x 19 x 369	Cherry
10	H	Case divdr ends	14 x 19 x 292	Cherry
2	I	Drawer sides	6 x 25 x 275	Maple
1	J	Drawer back	6 x 25 x 348	Maple
2	K	Drawer sides	6 x 35 x 275	Maple
1	L	Drawer back	6 x 35 x 348	Maple
2	M	Drawer sides	6 x 41 x 275	Maple
1	N	Drawer back	6 x 41 x 348	Maple
4	O	Drawer sides	6 x 54 x 275	Maple
2	P	Drawer backs	6 x 54 x 348	Maple
5	Q	Drawer bottoms	3 x 272 x 348	Masonite
7	R	Drawer dividers	3 x 13 x 262	Maple
7	S	Drawer dividers	3 x 10 x 341	Maple
7	T	Drawer dividers	3 x 25 x 362	Maple
5	U	Drawer dividers	3 x 16 x 341	Maple
2	V	Drawer dividers	3 x 32 x 262	Maple
2	W	Drawer dividers	3 x 25 x 341	Maple
4	X	Drawer dividers	3 x 38 x 262	Maple
2	Y	Drawer dividers	3 x 32 x 341	Maple
1	Z	Top	10 x 267 x 356	Maple
1	AA	Top trim	6 x 10 x 356	Maple

should meet at the inside miter of the sides. Trim the panel to fit. Then, using biscuits, glue the panel to the back and side pieces, also gluing the frame divider into the bottom rabbet. Checking for square is very important here. Continue to glue the other boxes together with their individual dividers. Tape in the drawer fronts for proper spacing here. The divider on the bottom box forms the base of the finished case. When dry, biscuit and glue the five layers of boxes together to form the finished case.

Airtight Drawers

For the drawers, it's best to first cut long strips to the width and thickness of the drawer pieces. Next cut the $1/8$" $\times$ $1/8$" rabbet in the bottom edge of each drawer blank. Crosscut the drawer parts to length according to the cutting list, then cut a $1/8$" $\times$ $1/8$" rabbet on the front end of each drawer side and on both ends of the drawer backs, leaving a $1/8$" $\times$ $1/4$" long tenon. On each side piece, cut a $1/8$" notch out of the top of each tenon to allow a shoulder to hide the mortise that follows. Cut corresponding dadoes into the back ends of the drawer sides to capture the back tenons.

Routing the mortises in the drawer fronts is a little tricky. Set up a router with a $1/8$" straight bit set for a $1/4$" depth. Clamp a straight-edge perpendicular to the drawer front as a guide in routing the stopped mortises. Locate the mortises so the drawer sides will be $1/32$" in from the inside edge of the end miters, so the drawers will be easier to fit. Rout the dadoes on each end of each drawer front, stopping $1/8$" from the top edge on the fronts. When you're happy with the fit of each drawer, glue them together. Traditional clamps proved cumbersome on this project. Just use plain masking tape to pull the joints together. Generate pressure on the joint by securing the tape to one part and then pulling it across the joint and sticking it to the other side. If everything works well, the drawers shouldn't require much fitting when dry.

The next step is to fit the drawer bottoms into the rabbets in the drawers. When fit, glue velvet to the bottoms and trim the edges flush. Next, place the bottoms back in the drawers, and using a sharp knife, trim the velvet where it meets the drawer side. Take the bottoms out and

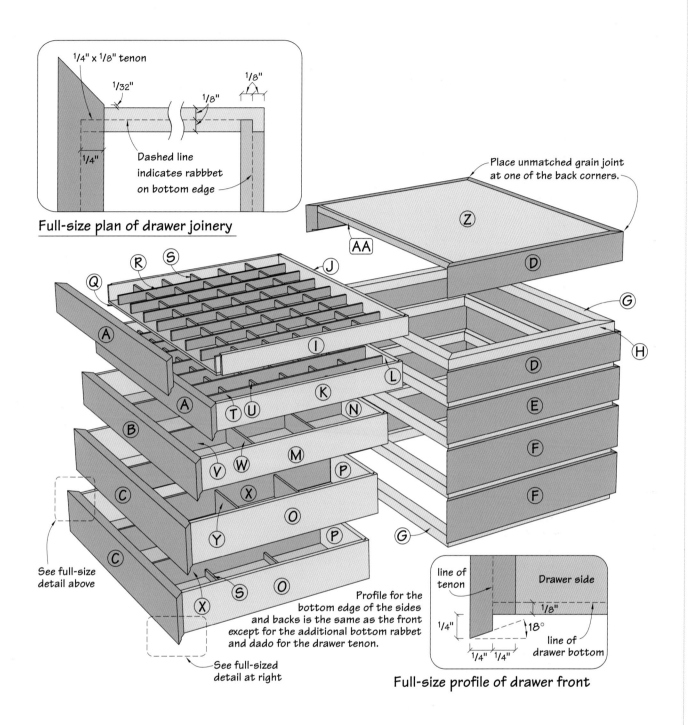

Full-size plan of drawer joinery

1/4" x 1/8" tenon

1/32"

1/8"

1/8"

1/4"

Dashed line
indicates rabbbet
on bottom edge

Place unmatched grain joint
at one of the back corners.

See full-size
detail above

See full-sized
detail at right

Profile for the
bottom edge of the sides
and backs is the same as the front
except for the additional bottom rabbet
and dado for the drawer tenon.

Full-size profile of drawer front

line of
tenon

Drawer side

1/8"

1/4"

18°

line of
drawer bottom

1/4"   1/4"

peel off the excess velvet. Glue the
bottoms back in after finishing.

The internal dividers are joined using
a cross-lap joint and placed in the drawer
after it's finished. Friction holds them in
place. When you're happy with the fit of
all the parts, sand to 220 grit and put three
coats of clear finish on the piece. Rub out
the finish using an extra-fine synthetic
steel wool and steel wool wax. Rub with
the grain and be careful not to rub through
the finish at the edges and corners. ■

photo
screen

Here's an interesting way to display your photos and brighten up that unused corner in your house.

IT'S GETTING HARDER AND HARDER THESE days to find ways to display your photos so you can generate interest in seeing them. When I was a kid, my parents would hang a large number of photos, gallery style, on a wall just to get them out in the open. Most of the time guests would look at the dizzying array of photos for a moment and ask my mother just how many children she really had (there was only my sister and me). This screen can generate interest and serve as a useful divider in your living space without taking up a lot of wall space.

THAT SAID, THERE ARE MANY photo arrangement combinations available for this screen. I simply made the one that worked best for me. Just add 1¼" to the picture size and you have your frame size using the moulding profile supplied in the diagrams.

This project will test your ability to make many small parts, but the payoff is worth it. I've found the best way around the tedium involved in repetitive operations is to challenge yourself to find the fastest way to do an individual operation and stick to it.

Make the Screen

Before cutting the panels out, let's talk about plywood selection. When you purchase the ply for this project, you want to make sure you get a nice sheet of material. Look for bookmatched veneer panels with a pattern centered on the 4' × 8' sheet. Start by cutting out the parts according to the cutting list. Crosscut the sheet first, then lay out the cuts for the panel rips.

Edge Taping

Lay out and cut the radiused corners on the outside panels and cut out the 6"-radius semicircles on the bottom of the panels. After cleaning up these cuts, apply heat-sensitive edge tape to all of the panels. File the edge tape flush, and finish sand the panels to 220 grit.

An Arc on Top

The distinctive arced trim on top of the screen is simply a lamination of three pieces of thinner wood, cut at the panel joints and doweled in place on top of the screen. Begin making the arc by milling out blanks of maple and cherry a little larger than the size given in the cutting list. Lay out the arc using the method suggested in the caption. Cut the arcs out on the band saw and sand the edges. Finish sand to 220 grit, and find a spot to do the laminating.

Start by making sure that your work surface is clean and flat. Mark the centers of each arc on its bottom edge. I used a fast-tack glue to laminate the arcs. This worked well because the glue has a short open time and you don't have to put a lot on the surface to get a good joint. Apply glue, and line up the three pieces with the

cutting list (inches): *photo screen*

No.	Item	Dimensions T W L	Material
3	Panels	¾" x 15" x 60"	Birch plywood
1	Arc cap	⅜" x 7½" x 40"	Cherry
2	Arc caps	⅛" x 5½" x 34"	Maple
1	Medallion	¼" x 4" diameter	Cherry
10	Large frame pieces	⅝" x ¾" x 11¼"	Cherry
10	Large frame pieces	⅝" x ¾" x 9¼"	Cherry
24	Small frame pieces	⅝" x ¾" x 8¼"	Cherry
24	Small frame pieces	⅝" x ¾" x 6¼"	Cherry
12	Face Plexiglas	⅛" x 5¼" x 7¼"	Plexiglas
5	Face Plexiglas	⅛" x 8¼" x 10¼"	Plexiglas
2	Spacers	½" x 2⅞" x 8"	Plywood
2	Spacers	½" x 1⅞" x 8"	Plywood
2	Spacers	½" x ⅞" x 8"	Plywood

cutting list (millimeters): *photo screen*

No.	Item	Dimensions T W L	Material
3	Panels	19 x 381 x 1524	Birch plywood
1	Arc cap	10 x 191 x 1016	Cherry
2	Arc caps	3 x 140 x 864	Maple
1	Medallion	6 x 102mm dia.	Cherry
10	Large frame pieces	16 x 19 x 285	Cherry
10	Large frame pieces	16 x 19 x 235	Cherry
24	Small frame pieces	16 x 19 x 209	Cherry
24	Small frame pieces	16 x 19 x 158	Cherry
12	Face Plexiglas	3 x 133 x 184	Plexiglas
5	Face Plexiglas	3 x 209 x 260	Plexiglas
2	Spacers	13 x 73 x 203	Plywood
2	Spacers	13 x 47 x 203	Plywood
2	Spacers	13 x 22 x 203	Plywood

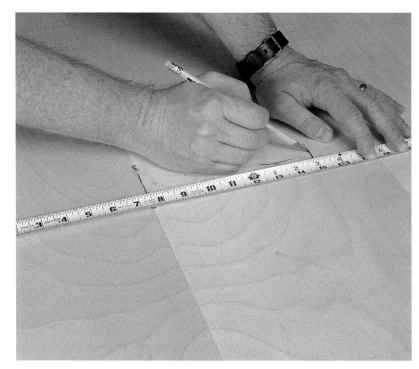

1 After crosscutting the panel to length, begin laying out the rip cuts by finding the center mark of the bookmatched veneer pattern. Lay out the center panel first and then the outer panels.

wood words

BOOKMATCHED: A method of arranging two consecutive slices of veneer, turning one over and laying them side by side, producing a mirror image, like the pages of a book.

FAST-TACK: Referring to glue that is a little thicker and has a shorter open time than other woodworking glues. In short, it gets stickier, faster. Sometimes called moulding glue.

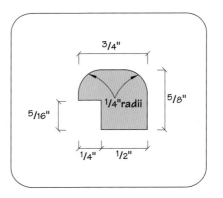

Profile of frame moulding

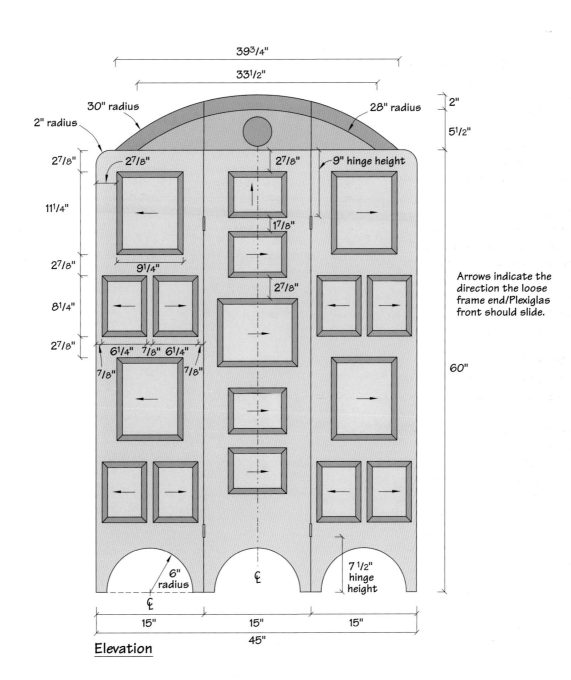

Arrows indicate the direction the loose frame end/Plexiglas front should slide.

Elevation

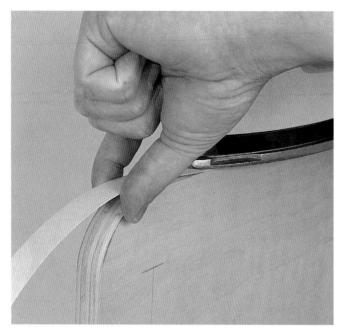

2 The proper way to iron on edge taping is to heat the tape with a household iron (don't tell your spouse you're doing this) and apply pressure with a roller while the hot melt glue is still soft.

3 The easiest way to make this radius is to get a piece of butcher paper for layout. Lay down a center line, and mark a square line at one end. Mark off the two radii from this mark as well as the two trim heights. Determine the bottom edge of the wood trim, and set it on the appropriate trim height mark. Using trammel points, lay out the radius according to the diagram.

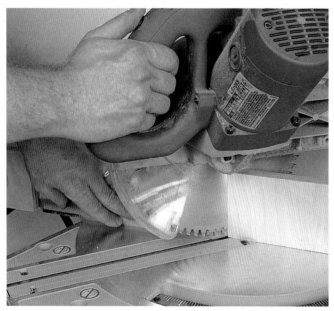

4 Setting your miter saw to the left will decrease kickbacks when making repetitive cuts. Screw a piece of plywood across the blade as a fence, and cut through it with your saw set to 45°. Measure from the inside of the miter cut to the left for the four different lengths. Cut the longest lengths first.

5 The object is to nail down three pieces with some of that fast-tack glue and leave the fourth side loose so it can slide out when the Plexiglas is attached. All of the loose sides on the panels should slide to the left or right. It doesn't matter which way, just that you can get past the double-swinging hinge barrel when you slide out the Plexi-frame end. The only exception was the top frame on the middle panel, which slides up.

6 Take the fourth frame piece and attach it to the Plexiglas with cyanoacrylate glue while it is in place. Gently pull the frame piece and Plexiglas assembly out of the frame.

center line flush on the bottom edge. Place the first clamp on the center with a backing strip of wood. Add more clamps as needed. Make sure to check the bottom edge for slippage and adjust accordingly. When the glue is dry, clean off the bottom edge and joint if necessary. Apply the 4" medallion to the front of the arc with glue and small nails.

On your work surface, place the panels together as they would be attached. Place the arc on the top edge and center it on the assembly. Mark where the joints are, and follow them to the top edge of the arc. Using a handsaw, cut the arc into three pieces. Clean up the sawn edges with a block plane, and dowel the pieces into their respective panels. You can glue these arc sections in or leave them loose. I left mine loose to make it easy to move the screen. Apply two coats of clear finish to all the panels and arc sections. Go ahead and rout the notches for the double-swinging hinges and attach them.

Cutting Moulding

After attaching the hinges, set the screen aside. Make the moulding according to the diagram. It takes about five 8' lengths to make all of the moulding. After sanding, apply two coats of clear finish to the moulding stock. Take the moulding that you made and begin cutting the frame parts as shown in the photo. After setting your chop saw to 45°, make the first miter cut by trimming the end of a long piece of moulding with the top down and the rabbet against the fence. Then turn the moulding around with the rabbet facing you. Put the piece against your stop and make the second cut. Be careful and accurate. Your results will speak for themselves. Never get complacent in these repetitive operations, and pay attention to where the saw blade is at all times. Safety first.

Nailing the Frames

After the frame pieces are cut, lay the screen on a flat, soft surface such as a piece of cardboard or a blanket. Begin laying out the frame locations according to the diagram. To make this easier, cut the spacers in the cutting list to locate the first two frame pieces in each frame. Attach the frames as shown in photo 6.

Mount a Picture

After mounting all the frames, it's time to attach the Plexiglas to the loose frame parts. Stand the screen upright for installing the Plexiglas. This lets the Plexiglas settle into the frame. Check to make sure that the Plexiglas fits into the opening in the frame piece. Next, slide a piece of cardboard into the opening. Peel back the protective plastic that covers the front of the Plexiglas and insert it into the frame. Shim it out until it is pushed all the way forward in the frame. Mount as shown in photo 6.

Finally, if you need to place a photo only, cut out a cardboard backer to fill the opening. If you have a matted photo, simply make sure that the matte fits the opening. ■

supplies

Woodcraft, www.woodcraft.com (800) 225-1153

- 4 - Double-swing hinges, item# 27G33, $3.75/pair
- Edge tape, item# 123273 ($14.99)

Available at most large hardware stores (Home Depot, Lowe's, etc.)

- Plexiglas

compact
ENTERTAINMENT
UNIT

A media center doesn't have to cover your entire wall. Sometimes smaller is better.

IT'S ALL THE RAGE TO BUILD ENTERTAINMENT centers that look like armoires. But sometimes an enormous cabinet is more than a room can handle. That was exactly the problem of the young couple I built this piece for.

They had purchased a large entertainment unit for their new home that overpowered the corner where it was supposed to stand. After looking at their living room and a few photos of traditional furniture they liked, we came up with this design for a compact entertainment unit that fit their spacious living room and their budget.

This traditional-looking piece is made from solid hardwood, though you could substitute veneered plywood for the sides, bottom and back. There is no fancy joinery in this cabinet. The case is built using dadoes and screws. The face frame is put together using mortises and tenons. The raised-panel doors are built the same way. The top is screwed to the case.

That said, there are a few good tricks you can pick up here. One is the way I fit the face frame to the case. I'll show you how to make it perfect the first time by making it a bit oversized. And I'll also show you some tricks for fitting inset doors that I've developed during my years as a cabinetmaker.

Begin With the Case

If you are going to use solid wood for this project, first glue up the panels for the sides, bottom and top. Clamp and allow them to dry. Then start milling the parts. Cut a ³⁄₄"-wide by ⅛"-deep dado in the sides to hold the bottom. For the back, cut a ¼" × ½" rabbet on the back edge of the sides. Now is a good time to drill the holes for the adjustable shelf pins. There's only one adjustable shelf in this project; you could add a second if it suits your electronic components.

Now assemble the case. I glued the bottom into the dado and then ran pocket screws through the bottom and into the sides.

Make sure the bottom piece is flush to the front edge of the sides. Then screw a stretcher between the sides. This stretcher is located at the rear of the cabinet and is

flush to the top and the inside of the back rabbet on the sides. The back pieces rest against this piece and the back edge of the bottom shelf when you install them at the end.

Face Frame

Face frames can be tricky to fit. If they shift the tiniest bit when you attach them, you can be in big trouble. Here's how to avoid that problem: When you rip the face frame stiles to their finished width, add ¹⁄₁₆" to the width. This will make your face frames overhang the sides slightly. So if the face frame shifts when it's attached, you can relax. Use your router and a flush-trimming bit to flush the face frame with the case. It's a simple but effective trick.

Build the face frame using mortise-and-tenon joinery. My tenons are ³⁄₈" thick and 1" long. I cut my tenons on the table saw

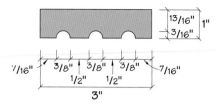

Plan detail of column fluting

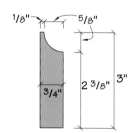

Detail profile of moulding

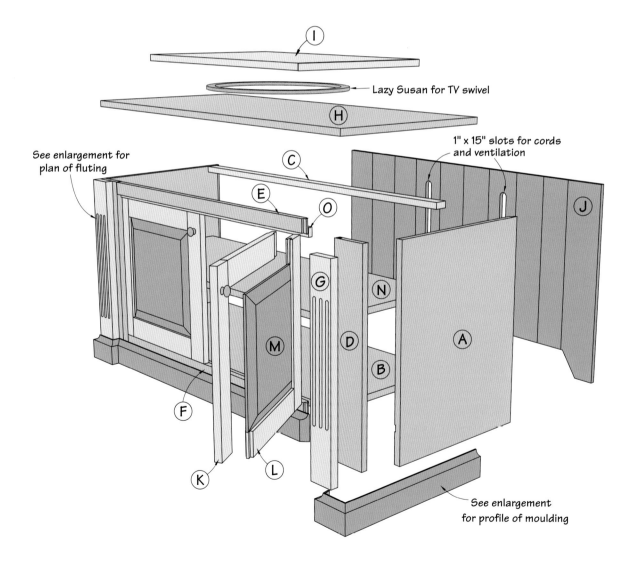

Lazy Susan for TV swivel

1" x 15" slots for cords and ventilation

See enlargement for plan of fluting

See enlargement for profile of moulding

1 Glue and nail, yes nail, the face frame to the case. The nail holes will be covered by the fluted columns later. Here you can see how the face frame slightly overhangs the case. I'll trim that later for a perfect fit.

2 After I cut the grooves on the stiles and rails of the door, I cut the mortises using this monstrous General mortiser (which is a joy to use) or a drill press and chisel will work just fine.

4 Cut the flutes using a fluting bit in your router. If you think you'll ever make fluted columns again, make a template like this one to quickly set up your fence next time.

3 Here you can see how the haunched tenon fits into the mortise and groove in the door's stiles. This sound and traditional joint will last a long time.

5 Use glue and clamps to attach the fluted columns to the face frame. I use little scraps of wood to prevent my bar clamps from marring the surface of my work.

supplies

Rockler, www.rockler.com, (800) 279-4441
- 4 - non-mortising hinges, item# 31482, $5.78 a pair
- 1 - Lazy Susan, item # 28894, $17.69 each

Horton Brasses, www.horton-brasses.com, (800) 754-9127
- 2 - knobs, item# K-12 w/MSF (machine screw fitting), call for pricing

6 Here you can see my shims at work. These hold the door in place for final fitting. I highly recommend you make some of these.

7 It's a good thing we eat a lot of popsicles at our house. I use the sticks to space my back pieces. You can also see the stretcher in action in this photo.

using a stack dado. Here's an unusual trick to avoid blowing out the shoulder when cutting your tenons on your table saw. First cut the ends of the tenons with the dado stack as you normally would, leaving about $\frac{1}{4}$" before the shoulder. Then make the final shoulder cut by pulling the wood back over the blade toward you. It sounds scary, but if you're careful it's not difficult, and it really does minimize tear-out.

Glue and clamp the face frame and allow it to dry. Nail and glue the face frame to the carcass. The nail holes will be covered by the fluted faux columns you'll attach later. Nail the door stop to the back of the top rail.

Make the Doors

The raised-panel doors are built using haunched tenons. First cut the 1"-long tenons on the rails. I cut the $\frac{3}{8}$" haunch on my table saw using a stack dado. Now cut the $\frac{3}{8}$" $\times$ $\frac{3}{8}$" groove on the inside edge of the rails and stiles using a dado stack in your table saw. Cut the $\frac{3}{8}$"-wide by 1"-deep mortises centered on the groove. Now raise the $\frac{5}{8}$"-thick panel. I like to remove most of the wood with my table saw, then finish the cut on my router or shaper with an 8° vertical panel-raising bit. This prevents me from having to reset the fence on my router table or shaper for two or more passes.

Now glue up the doors. Make sure you don't put any glue in the groove. You want the panels to float there.

Trim Out the Cabinet

First finish sand the entire cabinet inside and out. Then cut the $\frac{3}{8}$"-wide $\times$ $\frac{3}{16}$"-deep flutes in the columns using a fluting bit in your router table. Glue the columns to the case. Cut a $\frac{1}{2}$" $\times$ $\frac{1}{2}$" cove on the base moulding. Miter and attach it to the front and sides of the case.

Cut a roundover on the top and bottom edge of the top and attach it to the case using slotted screw pockets, cleats or whatever method you prefer.

Now add the $\frac{1}{2}$"-thick back pieces. Each piece has a $\frac{1}{2}$"-wide by $\frac{1}{4}$"-deep rabbet on each side (except the two end pieces, which have a rabbet on only one edge). I also cut a small bead on the long edges using a beading bit in my router. This rabbet allows you to shiplap the

pieces and allows for seasonal expansion and contraction. Sand the pieces and nail them into place.

Fit the Doors and Finish

I build my doors the same size as their opening and then trim them down to size on my jointer. This assures a perfect fit if the face frame or door is slightly out of square. Here's how to do it. First fit the door's hinge stile against the face frame stile and note where the door's rails and face frame rails are not parallel. Mark this information on the door.

Now set your jointer to make a $\frac{1}{32}$" cut. Cut the excess from the door by starting the cut in the middle of the door rail where the excess begins. Then clean up

that cut by making a second pass on your jointer that runs the entire length of the door. Next fit the door using $\frac{1}{16}$"-thick shims all around. You can make shims like this out of wood. Attach the doors to the face frame using non-mortise hinges.

One last detail before finishing. Attach the Lazy Susan to the board beneath the TV. I decided not to screw the Lazy Susan to the cabinet because who knows what this cabinet will become in its next life. Instead, I attached some of those clear adhesive door bumpers to the underside of the Lazy Susan and set it in place on top of the cabinet. It works great.

The finish is simple. Apply three coats of clear lacquer, sanding between each coat. ■

cutting list (inches): *compact entertainment unit*

No.	Ltr.	Item	Dimensions T W L	Material
2	A	Sides	$\frac{3}{4}$" x $18\frac{1}{2}$" x $23\frac{1}{4}$"	Cherry
1	B	Bottom	$\frac{3}{4}$" x 18" x $42\frac{1}{4}$"	Maple
1	C	Stretcher	$\frac{3}{4}$" x $1\frac{1}{2}$" x 42"	Maple
2	D	Face stiles	$\frac{3}{4}$" x 4" x $23\frac{1}{4}$"	Cherry
1	E	Top rail	$\frac{3}{4}$" x $1\frac{1}{2}$" x $37\frac{1}{2}$"	Cherry
1	F	Bottom rail	$\frac{3}{4}$" x 4" x $37\frac{1}{2}$"	Cherry
2	G	Columns	1" x 3" x $23\frac{1}{4}$"	Cherry
1	H	Top	$\frac{3}{4}$" x 21" x 45"	Cherry
1	I	TV base	$\frac{3}{4}$" x 17" x $27\frac{3}{4}$"	Cherry
	J	Back-boards	$\frac{1}{2}$" x $23\frac{1}{4}$" x $42\frac{1}{4}$"	Maple
4	K	Door stiles	$\frac{3}{4}$" x $2\frac{1}{2}$" x $17\frac{3}{4}$"	Cherry
4	L	Door rails	$\frac{3}{4}$" x $2\frac{1}{2}$" x $14\frac{3}{4}$"	Cherry
2	M	Door panels	$\frac{5}{8}$" x $13\frac{1}{4}$" x $13\frac{1}{2}$"	Cherry
1	N	Adjustable shelf	$\frac{3}{4}$" x $17\frac{3}{4}$" x $41\frac{3}{4}$"	Maple
1	O	Door stop	$\frac{1}{2}$" x 1" x $35\frac{1}{2}$"	Cherry

8' of 3"-wide moulding

cutting list (millimeters): *compact entertainment unit*

No.	Ltr.	Item	Dimensions T W L	Material
2	A	Sides	19 x 470 x 590	Cherry
1	B	Bottom	19 x 457 x 1073	Maple
1	C	Stretcher	19 x 38 x 1067	Maple
2	D	Face stiles	19 x 102 x 590	Cherry
1	E	Top rail	19 x 38 x 953	Cherry
1	F	Bottom rail	19 x 102 x 953	Cherry
2	G	Columns	25 x 76 x 590	Cherry
1	H	Top	19 x 533 x 1143	Cherry
1	I	TV base	19 x 432 x 705	Cherry
	J	Back-boards	13 x 590 x 1073	Maple
4	K	Door stiles	19 x 64 x 451	Cherry
4	L	Door rails	19 x 64 x 375	Cherry
2	M	Door panels	16 x 336 x 343	Cherry
1	N	Adjustable shelf	19 x 451 x 1060	Maple
1	O	Door stop	13 x 25 x 902	Cherry

2.5m of 76mm-wide moulding

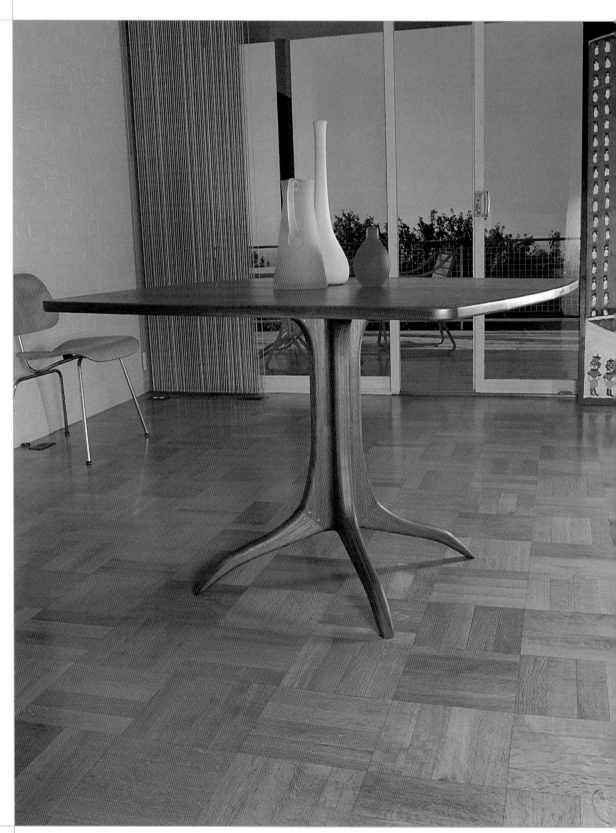

SCULPTED-BASE TABLE

"A craftsman must respect his material. How much more meaningful it becomes if one wears a bit of humility that allows him to acknowledge that it is truly God who is the Master Craftsman. He uses us. Our hands are His instruments."

— SAM MALOOF

ONE OF THE EARLIEST "HOW-TO" PROJECTS in *Popular Woodworking* (which at the time was called *Pacific Woodworker*) had the distinction of being a table made by renowned woodworker Sam Maloof. While the article was not an actual step-by-step explanation (indeed, there weren't even dimensions offered), the process for constructing the distinctive table base was described. Using that article, I built this Maloof-style table. And while this isn't a weekend project, it's not a particularly difficult piece. More importantly, this table will remind you of why you love to work with wood.

If you're concerned about copying another person's design, keep in mind what Maloof said in his book *Sam Maloof, Woodworker* when asked about those who copy his furniture:

"This reminds me of an anecdote about Hamada, the Japanese potter. When someone asked Hamada if imitations of his work bothered him, he replied, 'When I'm dead, people will think that all of my bad things were made by the other potter, and they will think that all of his good things were made by me.'"

Starting at the Post

The first step is roughing out and shaping the base's center post. The post measures $3" \times 3" \times 23"$, and unless you're very lucky you'll have to glue up a couple boards to achieve this dimension. Using $1\frac{3}{4}"$-thick material, I was able to glue up two $3"$-wide pieces with room to spare.

If you've ever tried to glue two flat pieces together, you know that glue works like butter, and the wood wants to slip apart. Drill two dowel holes on the matching faces, and use dowels as guide pins during gluing so you won't fight with your pieces.

Next mill the post down to $3" \times 3"$. You should leave the post longer than the finished $23"$ for now to allow for fitting. The first milling procedure is to use a dado stack to cut grooves the length of the post on all four faces.

Forming the Inside Curve

With the post grooved to accept the leg tenons, make cove cuts on the four corners so that the shape flows into the legs. I accomplished this with a $\frac{3}{4}"$ cove bit. This bit is a $50 necessity. There is no other tooling that provides the control given by a router and bit set up in a router table.

As shown in photo 2, the location of the cove cut is critical to how easy it will be to assemble the base and how good it will look. Use two passes of increasing depth to put less stress on your router.

Quite a Joint!

With the post essentially complete, it's time to make the legs. You will be making four duplicate leg sections, each made of three pieces.

Cut the pieces to rough size, being careful to mark the 45° angle location exactly. On each leg's top and center pieces you still have a flat edge to use as a guide to cut the angles on your table saw or power miter box. On each leg's bottom you'll need to make the cut with the band saw or a handsaw and sand the face flat. These are critical joints that determine how flat your table will sit, so pay special attention to making them meet correctly.

With the pieces roughed to shape, make the two rabbet cuts on the leg centers to leave a $1\frac{1}{16}" \times \frac{3}{4}"$-wide tenon. Check the fit with the grooves in the post.

1 The $\frac{3}{4}" \times \frac{3}{4}"$ grooves must be centered in the width of the post to make the fit (and the sanding) acceptable. A careful setup with a dado set makes this quick work.

2 Getting the cove cuts to align with the edges of the leg centers makes sanding and the final finish easier. If anything, allow the cove cuts to be a hair wider than necessary so that the sanding to fit occurs on the leg centers, not in the cove cut.

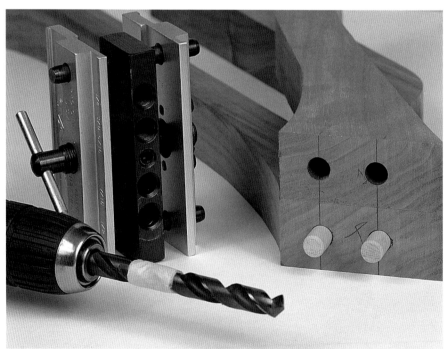

3 Use dowels to join the leg tops and bottoms to the leg center. I used $\frac{1}{2}"$ dowels, which were later pinned through the side of the legs with $\frac{1}{8}"$ dowels. A self-centering doweling jig like the one shown in the photo takes some of the measuring out of this step.

It should be a hand-tight fit.

Next sand the leg pieces to match the templates. A spindle sander is great for this step, but a drum sander chucked in your drill press will work, too. When you sand the shapes, leave a couple of inches to either side of each joint wide of the line. The joints should be shaped to match after the leg pieces have been glued together to ensure a smooth transition.

Lay out the locations for the ½" dowels as shown on the diagrams and in photo 3.

Clamping Ballet

The glue-up of the leg components is tricky, but photo 4 shows a method that worked well for me. Next, again look to the diagrams for the locations of the ⅛" dowels used to pin the larger dowels. Drill completely through the leg and dowel, but use a backing board to avoid tear-out on the exit side. Then add some glue to the 2" dowel lengths and tap them into place so the dowel protrudes on both sides. When the glue dries, sand the dowels flush.

With the pinning done, use a ½" roundover bit with a bearing guide to ease all the edges of each leg — except the

tenon edge and the top edge. Be careful while routing, especially at the joint, because the grain is likely to change direction and tear-out.

After routing, glue the legs to the center post. Definitely dry-fit the base

assembly, clamping the legs in place. Make sure the base sits flat without rocking, and mark the center post to cut it to length to match the legs. After that, glue and clamp the base.

cutting list (inches): *sam maloof's sculpted-base table*

No.	Ltr.	Item	Dimensions T W L	Material
1	A	Top	⅞" x 42" x 42"	Walnut
1	B	Post	3" x 3" x 23"	Walnut
4	C	Leg tops	1¾" x 2½" x 13½"	Walnut
4	D	Leg centers	1¾" x 2¾" x 23"	Walnut
4	E	Leg bottoms	1¾" x 3½" x 14½"	Walnut
2	F	Cross bands	¾" x ¾" x 5"	Maple
16	G	Dowels	½" x 2"	Maple
32	H	Dowels	⅛" x 2"	Maple

cutting list (millimeters): *sam maloof's sculpted-base table*

No.	Ltr.	Item	Dimensions T W L	Material
1	A	Top	22 x 1067 x 1067	Walnut
1	B	Post	76 x 76 x 584	Walnut
4	C	Leg tops	44 x 64 x 343	Walnut
4	D	Leg centers	44 x 70 x 584	Walnut
4	E	Leg bottoms	44 x 89 x 369	Walnut
2	F	Cross bands	19 x 19 x 127	Maple
16	G	Dowels	13 x 51	Maple
32	H	Dowels	3 x 51	Maple

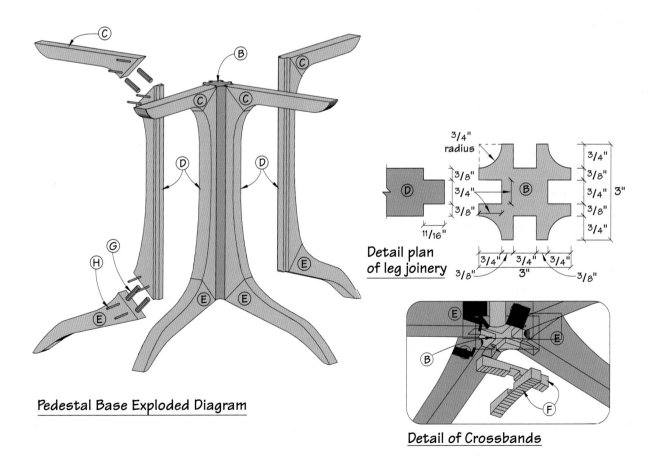

Pedestal Base Exploded Diagram

Detail plan of leg joinery

Detail of Crossbands

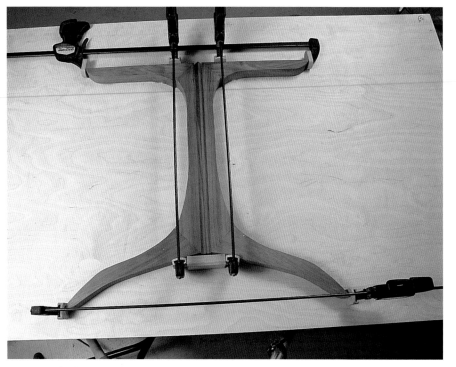

A Maloof Finish

Mix one-third semi-gloss polyurethane varnish, one-third pure tung oil and one-third boiled linseed oil. You can substitute linseed oil with another third tung oil if it is polymerized (pure tung oil dries too slowly). Apply this mixture three times at one-day intervals.

For a final coat, heat a 50/50 mix of pure tung oil and boiled linseed oil (or 100 percent polymerized tung oil) in a double boiler. Grate solid beeswax and add it to the heated mix until it is the consistency of heavy cream (about two double-handfuls of wax per gallon of mix). Let cool. The wax in the cooled mixture will stay in suspension and has a good shelf life. This is applied a minimum of three times, vigorously rubbing in the mixture each time.

4 Properly gluing and clamping the leg sections is awkward. The clamp arrangement shown here glued two leg sections at the same time with only four clamps. The block between the leg bottoms kept the clamps from sliding on the sculpted leg.

5 The half-lapped pieces of maple are shown in place (left), shaped, screwed and plugged. The process was more time consuming, but the finished appearance is dramatic. The photo above shows a recessed screw slot to attach the top to the base. Maloof's pieces would have been screwed then plugged.

Strength and a Decorative Touch

Before sanding, there is one detail Maloof adds to his sculpted-base tables that adds strength, as well as a nice touch.

The half-lapped maple cross pieces are added to provide strength across the base, tying the opposing legs together with the center post. Chisel the ¾" -wide by 5"-long grooves for the pieces to a depth of ½" at the center of the X, and allow the bottom of the groove to level out into the legs. This leaves the trench about ⅝" deep at the ends of the grooves.

Next cut the half-lap joint in the two maple pieces and fit them into the two grooves. Then drill four ⅛" pilot holes, ½" in from the ends of the pieces. Then drill ⅜" × ⅜" deep holes to allow the screw heads to recess into the maple. After inserting the four No. 8 × 2" flathead screws, plug the holes with ⅜" diameter walnut plugs.

After that, the rest is rasping and sanding. Maloof's pieces are known for their contours and smoothness of transitions. I honestly spent about six hours shaping and sanding the base through to 220 grit. It was worth the effort.

It seems silly, but the most visible part of the table took the least amount of effort. The 42" square/round top was made of four ⅞" × 11" walnut boards. I didn't want to use more than four boards for the top,

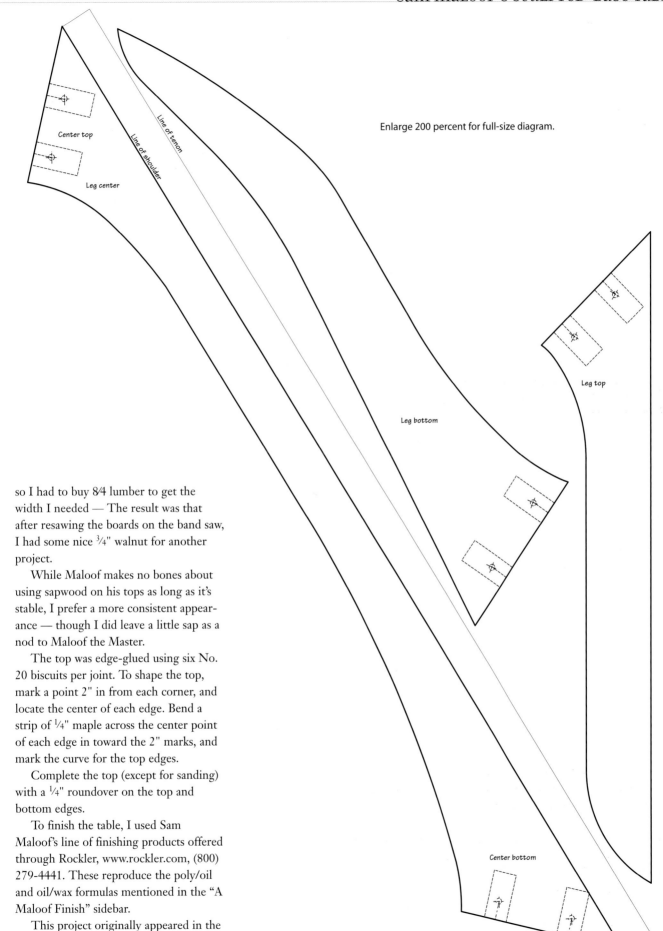

Center top

Leg center

Line of tenon

Line of shoulder

Enlarge 200 percent for full-size diagram.

Leg top

Leg bottom

Center bottom

so I had to buy 8/4 lumber to get the width I needed — The result was that after resawing the boards on the band saw, I had some nice 3/4" walnut for another project.

While Maloof makes no bones about using sapwood on his tops as long as it's stable, I prefer a more consistent appearance — though I did leave a little sap as a nod to Maloof the Master.

The top was edge-glued using six No. 20 biscuits per joint. To shape the top, mark a point 2" in from each corner, and locate the center of each edge. Bend a strip of 1/4" maple across the center point of each edge in toward the 2" marks, and mark the curve for the top edges.

Complete the top (except for sanding) with a 1/4" roundover on the top and bottom edges.

To finish the table, I used Sam Maloof's line of finishing products offered through Rockler, www.rockler.com, (800) 279-4441. These reproduce the poly/oil and oil/wax formulas mentioned in the "A Maloof Finish" sidebar.

This project originally appeared in the July 1982 issue of Pacific Woodworker. ■

kitchen ISLAND

There's never been enough space in the kitchen — until now!

I DON'T KNOW IF YOU'VE EVER SPENT A LOT of time in the kitchen (besides that time you used the dishwasher for that steam-bending experiment), but the number one complaint of cooks is the profound lack of space there — especially in homes built before the 1970s.

Short of tearing out a wall, this kitchen island is the best way to stretch your existing counter space by 7½ square feet and increase another commodity that's in short supply in many kitchens: storage space. And on those nights you're eating grilled cheese for dinner instead of lobster thermidor and don't need the extra space, the kitchen island rolls into a corner out of the way.

This kitchen island is made of hard maple and maple-veneered MDF (medium-density fiberboard). To make things easier, I didn't build the maple butcher-block top. You can make your own, buy it from a local vendor or order it cut to size from the distributor listed at the end of the article.

Legs, Sides and Shelves

Cut the 2" stock for the legs to the size listed in the cutting list. Then cut all the case parts from ¾" MDF maple plywood. Now cut the 7" × 13¼" notches in the sides for the shelves and onion bin. You'll notice that I made the grain on the sides run left-to-right. Because wood movement isn't a problem with MDF, you can make the grain run whatever direction you want.

The inner bottom below the drawers is biscuited into the sides and back so it fits flush to the bottom of the notches in the sides. I then cut ¼"-deep × ½"-wide grooves and rabbets into the sides and back to capture the two tray dividers. The lower divider is captured flush to the bottom of the case sides in the rabbet, then the groove is cut 1½" up from the top of the rabbet. The corners of the tray dividers will need to be notched to fit into the corners, but it's best to do that after your first dry assembly. For now, make all your cuts,

but don't assemble anything yet, there's more to do.

Biscuit Joint Boogie

Lay out the biscuit locations to attach the legs to the back and side panels, holding the panels ½" in from the outside of the legs. With the notch in the side panels, there isn't a very long glue joint left at the rear legs. Fear not. After applying veneer edge tape to the edges of the notch, cut a filler to the size of each opening and tape it in place temporarily. This allows you to clamp evenly across the case, keeping the whole thing square when you glue together the case assembly later.

The inner construction of the case consists of three vertical panels: the center divider, the bin divider and the drawer divider. The bin and drawer divider are screwed in place through the center divider (see the plan view in the diagrams). Then the bin divider is biscuited into the case

back, while the center divider is biscuited between the two case sides, flush with the vertical edge of the notches. The inner bottom is then screwed to the dividers. Now iron on veneer edge tape to the front drawer divider and the case bottom.

Preparing the Legs

Next cut the notches in the legs to accommodate the front rail and the lower shelf. The top rail requires a ¾" × ¾" × 1½" squared-out notch. The one for the lower shelf is a little different. Start by laying out a ¾"-wide × 1½" notch on the two inside faces of all four legs, 2¾" up from the bottom. Starting your saw cut at the inside corner, define the top and bottom edges of the notch, cutting diagonally across the inside corner. Then remove the waste, leaving a triangular notch. The corners of the lower shelf are then cut at a 45° angle to fit into the notches.

cutting list **(inches):** *kitchen island*

No.	Item	Dimensions T W L	Material
1	Top	1½" x 24" x 30"	Maple
1	Drop Leaf	1½" x 10" x 30"	Maple
4	Legs	2" x 2" x 32¼"	Maple
2	Case sides	¾" x 18" x 18"	Plywood
1	Case back	¾" x 18" x 24"	Plywood
1	Inner bottom	¾" x 20¼" x 25½"	Plywood
2	Tray dividers	½" x 20½" x 26"	Plywood
1	Lower shelf	¾" x 21" x 27"	Plywood
1	Center divider	¾" x 13¼" x 25½"	Plywood
1	Bin divider	¾" x 13¼" x 7¾"	Plywood
2	Drawer divider	¾" x 13¼" x 11"	Plywood
1	Front rail	¾" x 3" x 25½"	Plywood
2	Drawer faces	¾" x 6¼" x 16¼"	Plywood
4	Drawer fronts	½" x 5¾" x 14¼"	Plywood
4	Drawer sides	½" x 5¾" x 10¾"	Plywood
2	Drawer backs	½" x 5" x 14¼"	Plywood
2	Drawer bottoms	¼" x 6¾" x 10½"	Plywood
3	Drawer faces	¾" x 4⅛" x 7¾"	Plywood
3	Drawer fronts	½" x 3½" x 6¾"	Plywood
2	Drawer sides	½" x 3½" x 10¾"	Plywood
2	Drawer backs	½" x 3" x 6¾"	Plywood
2	Drawer bottoms	¼" x 6¾" x 10½"	Plywood
4	Drawer cleats	¾" x 1½" x 10¼"	Plywood
1	Drawer cleat	½" x ½" x 10¼"	Plywood
1	Drawer cleat	¾" x 1½" x 13¼"	Plywood
2	Bin sides	½" x 13¼" x 16½"	Plywood
1	Bin back	½" x 12½" x 6½"	Plywood
1	Bin bottom	¼" x 16¼" x 6½"	Plywood
2	Bin face stiles	¾" x 1" x 13¼"	Maple
2	Bin face rails	¾" x 1" x 7"	Maple
5	Drawer fillers	¾" x 2" x 10"	Plywood
2	Bin Fillers	¾" x 2" x 15½"	Plywood

cutting list **(millimeters):** *kitchen island*

No.	Item	Dimensions T W L	Material
1	Top	38 x 610 x 762	Maple
1	Drop Leaf	38 x 254 x 762	Maple
4	Legs	51 x 51 x 819	Maple
2	Case sides	19 x 457 x 457	Plywood
1	Case back	19 x 457 x 610	Plywood
1	Inner bottom	19 x 514 x 648	Plywood
2	Tray dividers	13 x 521 x 660	Plywood
1	Lower shelf	19 x 533 x 686	Plywood
1	Center divider	19 x 336 x 648	Plywood
1	Bin divider	19 x 336 x 197	Plywood
2	Drawer divider	19 x 336 x 279	Plywood
1	Front rail	19 x 76 x 648	Plywood
2	Drawer faces	19 x 158 x 412	Plywood
4	Drawer fronts	13 x 146 x 362	Plywood
4	Drawer sides	13 x 146 x 273	Plywood
2	Drawer backs	13 x 127 x 362	Plywood
2	Drawer bottoms	6 x 171 x 267	Plywood
3	Drawer faces	19 x 105 x 197	Plywood
3	Drawer fronts	13 x 89 x 171	Plywood
2	Drawer sides	13 x 89 x 273	Plywood
2	Drawer backs	13 x 76 x 171	Plywood
2	Drawer bottoms	6 x 171 x 267	Plywood
4	Drawer cleats	19 x 38 x 260	Plywood
1	Drawer cleat	13 x 13 x 260	Plywood
1	Drawer cleat	19 x 38 x 336	Plywood
2	Bin sides	13 x 336 x 419	Plywood
1	Bin back	13 x 318 x 165	Plywood
1	Bin bottom	6 x 412 x 165	Plywood
2	Bin face stiles	19 x 25 x 336	Maple
2	Bin face rails	19 x 25 x 178	Maple
5	Drawer fillers	19 x 25 x 254	Plywood
2	Bin Fillers	19 x 51 x 394	Plywood

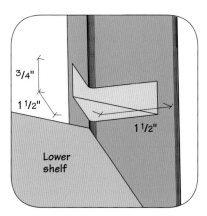

Detail of lower shelf notch

3/4"
1 1/2"
1 1/2"
Lower shelf

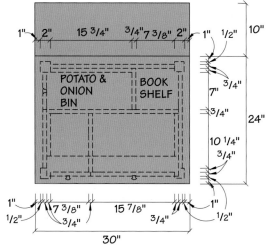

Plan

1" 2" 15 3/4" 3/4" 7 3/8" 2" 1" 1/2" 10"

POTATO & ONION BIN

BOOK SHELF

7"
3/4"
3/4"
24"
10 1/4"
3/4"

1" 7 3/8" 15 7/8" 1"
1/2" 3/4" 3/4" 1/2"
30"

1 The notches require four saw setups. The trick here is to keep the outside surface facing up when you're making these cuts. This will keep the blade undercut on the inside of your case piece, where it won't be seen. First, lay out the locations of the notches. Cut the second notch to allow the waste piece to fall to the waste side of the blade, so plan your cuts accordingly. Make the cuts with your saw blade up all the way.

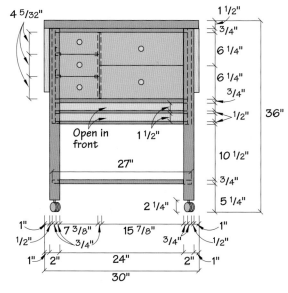

Elevation

4 5/32"
1 1/2"
3/4"
6 1/4"
6 1/4"
3/4"
1/2"
36"
Open in front
1 1/2"
27"
10 1/2"
3/4"
2 1/4"
5 1/4"

1" 7 3/8" 15 7/8" 1"
1/2" 3/4" 3/4" 1/2"
1" 2" 24" 2" 1"
30"

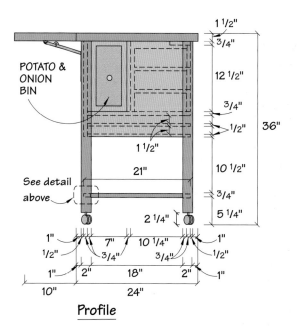

Profile

1 1/2"
3/4"
POTATO & ONION BIN
12 1/2"
3/4"
1/2"
36"
1 1/2"
See detail above
21"
10 1/2"
3/4"
2 1/4"
5 1/4"

1" 7" 10 1/4" 1"
1/2" 3/4" 3/4" 1/2"
1" 2" 18" 2" 1"
10" 24"

2 Joining material of different thicknesses with biscuits is easy when you use spacer blocks. Using a ³/₄" piece of MDF on top of my work put the biscuit slot in the middle of the panel without having to change the fence setting. After cutting the slot in the panel, I used the same setup to cut a slot in the legs.

3 The photo shows the cut for the top notch. Mark the location of the notch with a marking gauge, then cut across the diagonal to the center of the leg with a pullsaw. Finally, square out and clean the waste with a chisel.

Case Assembly

With the inner case assembled, it's time to dry-assemble the whole case. First, lay out and cut the ³/₄" × ³/₄" notches on the back corners and the ³/₄" × 1¹/₂" notches on the front corners of the inner bottom. Also, cut the 1" × 1" notches on the back corners and 1" × 1¹/₂" notches on the front corners of the tray dividers. Finally, lay out and cut 1¹/₂" × 1¹/₂" mitered corners on the lower shelf. You're now ready to dry assemble.

Begin by fitting the biscuits and dry-clamping the case back between the back legs flat on a bench. Then fit the inner case assembly to the back leg assembly with biscuits. Now set the sides into place on the back legs' respective joints.

With the front legs not in place yet, you should be able to slide the tray dividers and shelf into place. Then place the front legs in place and check for a good fit.

Disassemble the legs and case panels, and rout a ¹/₈" radius on all four long edges of the legs. Lastly, before gluing the unit together, screw and glue the cleats for attaching the top assembly to the sides. Wait until the case is assembled before attaching the

fillers for the drawer slides (see photo 4).

Proceed to glue up the case and legs. Check the case for square after assembly. As you begin to clamp the case together, remove the masking tape from the sides that will interfere with the glue joints. Now you can iron on veneer edge tape to the four edges of the bottom shelf and the fronts of the two tray dividers.

Build the drawers by first cutting out and assembling the sides, fronts and backs using simple glued-and-nailed rabbets for the joinery. The rabbet is ¹/₄" × ¹/₂". Make sure to check the sizes given with the

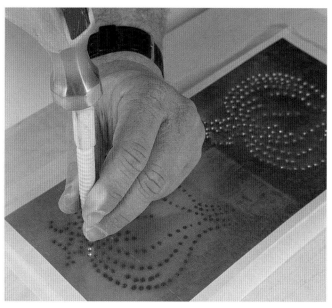

4 When the case is dry, install the filler blocking for the drawer slides. Use a block cut to the height you want your drawer slides to sit. Hold the spacer against the side, lay the filler strip on top of it and nail away! Always remember to attach the top blocking first then work your way down.

5 After some testing, the tool I liked best for punching the tin was a nail set with a fine tip. Make a copy of the pattern and tape it to a piece of tin cut to size. Center the pattern on the material and punch away.

6 The instructions offer different mounting locations for different setbacks on the sides. I chose 1 1/2" between the barrel of the hinge and the leaf. First attach the long end of the stay to the leaf. Then attach the short end to the case, 2 1/16" down from the top of the case, allowing the leaf to drop down all the way.

openings on the case as they may vary slightly. Also remember the large drawers use drawer slides that require the drawer boxes be 1" smaller in width than the opening. Cut out the drawer faces and edge tape them, then finish sand and set aside.

Build the Bin

Though similar in construction to the drawers, the bin front is a stile-and-rail frame built with half-lap joints. A punched tin panel is then nailed to the inside. Also, the front is the drawer face, and the entire bin fits inset in the opening, rather then overlaying.

The bin sides fit into 1/2" × 1/2" rabbets cut on the sides of the assembled bin front. Cut a 1/2" × 1/4" rabbet on the inside back edge of the sides to capture the bin back. Finally, make a 1/4" × 1/4" groove 1/4" up from the bottom edge of all four drawer pieces to capture the bottom. Now punch the pattern in the tin using the method shown in the photo, and nail the punched tin into the bin front after it's finished.

Attach the wooden knob to the bin by running a screw through a $\frac{3}{4}$" × $\frac{3}{4}$" × 6" wooden strip that is attached to the front frame of the bin, behind the tin.

Down to the Nitty Gritty

Cut the top and leaf as detailed in the cutting list. Ours was already finished with a catalyzed varnish. Begin attaching the top by laying the top and the leaf next to each other and attaching the continuous hinge to the top and leaf at the joint. Place the case upside-down on the top and locate it roughly in the center. At this point there should be about $1\frac{1}{2}$" between the back of the case and the hinge barrel. This is important for attaching the drop-leaf supports. Screw the case to the top with cleats, then attach the stays.

Flip the piece back over and place it on a level surface to attach the drawer faces. Start by placing the drawer boxes into their openings, then, using shims to locate the lower-left drawer face, clamp it to the box. Pull it out and hammer a couple short nails into the front from the inside of the box. This gives you a fairly adjustable drawer face. Repeat the process with the remaining fronts and then adjust the faces so there are equal gaps around each drawer. When done, drill a clearance hole in the front of the box and attach the faces with screws.

Now you're ready to finish the piece. Remove the drawer faces from the drawer boxes, and the top from the case. Finish sand all of the parts and finish the case with three coats of clear finish. Rubbing out the finish with a gray ScotchBrite pad and some wool wax soap will yield a stellar finish on this tight-grained maple.

When the finishing is done, reassemble the top and case upside-down, then drill the holes for the locking casters and install. Now you're ready to carve that pot roast. ■

supplies

Tamarack Distributors, (800) 582-4555
• 2 -25" x 30" butcher block slabs, $123.50

**Woodcraft, www.woodcraft.com
(800) 225-1153**
• Casters, item# 27I46, $9.50 for a set of four
• Drawer slides item# 27E30, $16.50/set

Woodworker's Supply, (800) 645-9292
• Stays, item# R11965, $12.50/pair

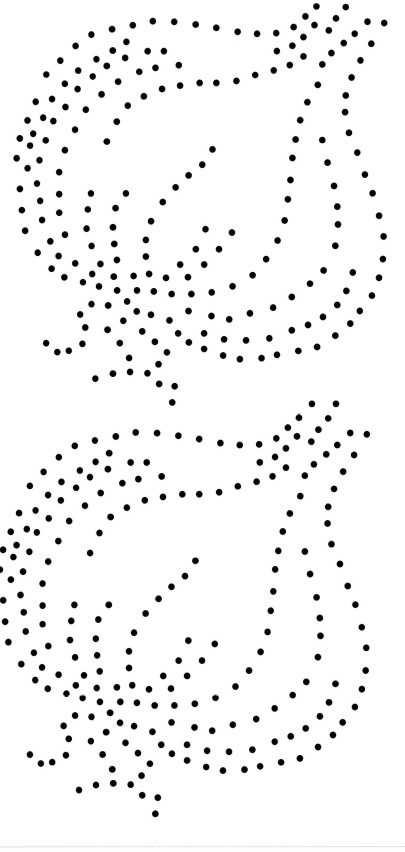

Full-size layout of the punched tin pattern. Note that the locations of each onion are where they should be positioned on the tin.

revolving
BOOKSHELF

ABOUT 1800 THE READING WORLD GOT A BIT lazy and decided it was too much trouble to walk across a room to grab a book from a built-in bookshelf. Along came a revolving bookshelf that sat next to the chair or desk. Since then, the space-saving benefits of the design have been employed for storing compact discs and videotapes, as well as books.

I took the idea further by adding a drawer and book stand, and went with a dramatic modern design.

Much of the piece is plywood, which is a good, affordable material for the black finish. The wood for the sides is sold as moradillo (or morado) at our lumber supplier, but we've had a hard time locating it anywhere else. A few well-selected boards of walnut would have almost the same effect.

BEGIN BY CUTTING ALL THE pieces as detailed in the cutting list. Construction is a little more complex than a simple box. The four centers are arranged into a plus sign (see the diagram). This plus sign is attached to the base at the bottom and to a box with a drawer at the top. The shelves are biscuited into the four centers and the outside panels are biscuited to the centers and the shelves. Most of the joinery for the project uses biscuits; dowels or carefully placed, set and plugged nails would work, too. To prepare the centers for assembly, first cut $3/4$"-wide by $3/8$"-deep grooves $3/4$" in from the back edge of each center piece on one face.

Now prepare the shelves and base piece. Cut about 12' of poplar edging $1/4$" × $13/16$" and crosscut the pieces to fit the front edge of each of the shelves and the four edges of the bottom. Glue the edges on and allow them to hang over on all four sides to allow for trimming.

Before any assembly, lay out the location for all the shelves, and mark and cut biscuit pockets. Each shelf has pockets on two long and one short edge. The lower shelf is 12" up from the bottom. The upper shelf is 10" up from that. Wait to cut the pockets in the sides until the inner section is assembled to check the locations.

With all the biscuit pockets cut, glue

and clamp the centers together to form the plus sign.

Next glue the shelves in place. When complete, center the assembly on the bottom and mark the location. Then remove the assembly, and drill two clearance holes per center panel in the bottom. Attach the bottom using No. 8 × $1 1/2$" flathead screws.

Now make the box that goes on top of the bookshelf. Locate and attach one of the inside tops to the top of the assembly as with the bottom. Use biscuits to assemble the drawer box atop the center assembly. The sides of the box should extend below the inside top by $1/8$". This will be important as the extra $1/8$" will serve as the finger pull for the drawer, so locate the biscuits accordingly. First biscuit and glue two corner blocks to the back piece, and one block each to the front end of each side piece. Then glue the two sides to the upper and lower inside top panels. Now glue the back in place.

Next build the drawer. I simply butt-nailed the ends between the sides. The bottom is captured in a $1/4$" groove cut $1/8$" up from the bottom of the sides and ends. Next, cut and fit the drawer front and screw it to the drawer. Check the fit between the two end blocks.

Next make the base. Cut the two base pieces to the shape shown in the diagram. Sand the pieces of the base and assemble with a $1 1/2$" flathead screw through the half-lap joint. Cut the book stop for the top and round over the two ends.

The top will be a book rest. It is hinged

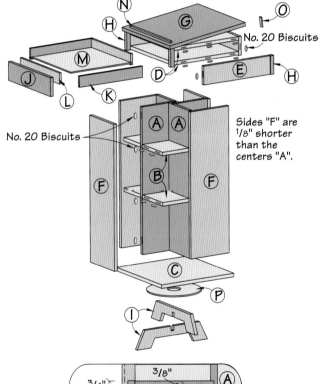

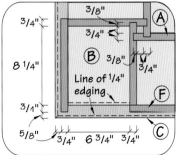

Detail of center assembly

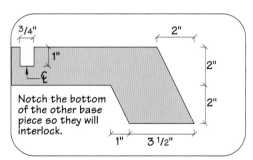

Detail of base cutout

Detail of support bracket and recess cut into the underside of the top (left), and hinge recess at the front. Hinged top is fully opened (right).

rounded end of recess

on one side. A hinged top support recessed into the underside of the top props up the top. Mark a $1\frac{1}{8}$" × $3\frac{1}{2}$" recess on the underside of the top 2" in from the top edge and centered side-to-side. Remove enough material to form the $\frac{5}{8}$"-deep recess (see photo). Then mount the support in the recess with a jewelrybox hinge. When the lid is laid flat, the support folds up invisibly under the top. The top itself is attached at the front two corner blocks by $\frac{1}{2}$" jewelrybox hinges mortised into the top of the blocks.

If you choose to use the black lacquer finish, now is the time to paint or spray. Tape off the corner blocks and the edges of the center panels and shelves where the side panels will attach. If these edges aren't taped off, the glue will not adhere properly when the sides are attached. Paint the case, the base and the book stop. Go ahead and paint the entire drawer, then add a couple coats of clear lacquer to protect the black finish.

Cut the biscuit slots on the inside of the moradillo panels. Tape over the glue locations on the panels and put a couple coats of clear finish on the loose side panels and on the top.

Assemble the bookcase; first attach the swivel plate to the base. Turn the bookcase upside down and attach the base and swivel. Remove the tape from the glue surfaces and glue the side panels to the case.

Depending on your finish, you might want to add another coat of clear finish to the assembled case at this time. Drill clearance holes through the top to attach the book stop, then attach the hinges and mount the top in place. ∎

cutting list **(inches):** *revolving bookshelf*

No.	Ltr.	Item	Dimensions T W L	Material
4	A	Centers	$\frac{3}{4}$" x $8\frac{5}{8}$" x $31\frac{1}{2}$"	Plywood
8	B	Shelves	$\frac{3}{4}$" x $6\frac{3}{4}$" x 8"*	Plywood
1	C	Bottom	$\frac{3}{4}$" x 18" x 18"*	Plywood
2	D	Inside tops	$\frac{3}{4}$" x 17" x 17"	Plywood
3	E	Upper sides	$\frac{3}{4}$" x 4" x 17"	Plywood
4	F	Sides	$\frac{3}{4}$" x $9\frac{3}{4}$" x $31\frac{3}{8}$"	Moradillo
1	G	Top	$\frac{3}{4}$" x $19\frac{1}{2}$" x $19\frac{1}{2}$"	Moradillo
4	H	Corner blocks	$\frac{7}{8}$" x $\frac{7}{8}$" x 4"	Moradillo
2	I	Base halves	$\frac{3}{4}$" x 4" x 18"	Poplar
1	J	Drawer front	$\frac{3}{4}$" x 4" x $16\frac{7}{8}$"	Poplar
2	K	Drawer sides	$\frac{1}{2}$" x $2\frac{3}{8}$" x 16"	Baltic ply
2	L	Drawer ends	$\frac{1}{2}$" x $2\frac{3}{8}$" x $15\frac{15}{16}$"	Baltic ply
1	M	Drawer bottom	$\frac{1}{4}$" x $15\frac{1}{2}$" x $16\frac{1}{2}$"	Plywood
1	N	Book stop	$\frac{1}{2}$" x $\frac{1}{2}$" x 12"	Poplar
1	O	Top support	$\frac{3}{8}$" x 1" x $2\frac{1}{2}$"	Moradillo
1	P	12" swivel platform		

*Size of the bottom and shelves before gluing on $\frac{1}{4}$"-thick solid poplar edging. The $6\frac{3}{4}$" edge on the shelves has edging. The bottom has edging glued to all four edges.

cutting list **(millimeters):** *revolving bookshelf*

No.	Ltr.	Item	Dimensions T W L	Material
4	A	Centers	19 x 219 x 800	Plywood
8	B	Shelves	19 x 171 x 203*	Plywood
1	C	Bottom	19 x 457 x 457*	Plywood
2	D	Inside tops	19 x 432 x 432	Plywood
3	E	Upper sides	19 x 102 x 432	Plywood
4	F	Sides	19 x 248 x 797	Moradillo
1	G	Top	19 x 496 x 496	Moradillo
4	H	Corner blocks	22 x 22 x 102	Moradillo
2	I	Base halves	19 x 102 x 457	Poplar
1	J	Drawer front	19 x 102 x 428	Poplar
2	K	Drawer sides	13 x 61 x 406	Baltic ply
2	L	Drawer ends	13 x 61 x 405	Baltic ply
1	M	Drawer bottom	6 x 394 x 419	Plywood
1	N	Book stop	13 x 13 x 305	Poplar
1	O	Top support	10 x 25 x 61	Moradillo
1	P	12" swivel platform		

*Size of the bottom and shelves before gluing on 6mm -thick solid poplar edging. The 171mm edge on the shelves has edging. The bottom has edging glued to all four edges.

jewelry
armoire

Classic styling masks the functionality of this tabletop keepsake.

THOUGH I'M VERY MUCH AWARE I NEVER will be able to make a jewelry box large enough to satisfy my wife's ambitions, I think I've finally made one attractive enough to keep her content.

This jewelry armoire uses clean, art deco styling and highly figured curly maple, accented with black lacquer. The most important aspect of this project is selecting a finely figured wood to serve as the focal point.

Select Your Wood

To achieve the most dramatic effect from the wood, I chose a single piece of curly maple that measured $8^{1}/_{2}$" across. This allowed me not only to cut all the drawer fronts from one piece, but also I was able to match the grain so it carried around the side of the door to the front. Construction is actually very simple. First cut all the parts as shown in the cutting list, marking the door and drawer parts to retain grain orientation. Then make the side dado cuts as shown in photo 1.

The door backs require a clearance cut to receive the mortise hinges, as detailed in photo 2. The drawer fronts receive similar cuts for the drawer pulls to fit flush with the top edge. Center these cuts and make them $^{1}/_{8}$" deep. Then cut the drawer pulls from a strip of poplar on the table saw, making a lip at the front of the pulls (see diagram detail).

The detail on the top and bottom of the armoire comes next (see photos 3 and 4).

Make the Doors

First sand all the interior surfaces of the door pieces, then glue the pieces of the doors together. Start with the door fronts and sides. Do each of these steps individually, because if you try to glue all the pieces in place at one time, you may end up with a horrible, sticky mess.

Spread the Glue

Once the door fronts are in place and the glue dries, glue the top and bottom pieces in place using the back pieces to gauge the spacing at the rear of the door. The final step is to glue the back pieces in place.

Drawer Assembly

Next, assemble the drawer boxes using finger, or box, joints. I used Baltic 5-ply plywood for the drawer sides. This material works well for strength, and it adds an attractive detail to the finger joints. After cutting the pieces, assemble as shown in photos 5 and 6.

Drawer Pulls

Finish all parts prior to assembly. Put masking tape on the drawer pull bottoms to leave bare wood for a better glue bond to the drawer front.

1 The case sides have $^{1}/_{4}$" dadoes cut on the insides to accept the drawer bottoms, which do double duty as drawer slides. Starting from the bottom edge of the sides, cut the dadoes at $2^{7}/_{8}$", $5^{3}/_{8}$", $7^{5}/_{8}$", $9^{5}/_{8}$" and $11^{5}/_{8}$". Also cut a $^{1}/_{4}$" x $^{1}/_{4}$" rabbet on the inside rear edges to receive the back.

2 I mortised the door back pieces for the three $^{1}/_{8}$"-thick hinges used on each door. The hinges you use may be different, so I won't bother giving you their cutting locations. To mill the relief cuts, I made repeat passes over the saw blade using my slot miter gauge to guide the work.

3 Create the step detail on the top and bottom pieces using four saw setups. The first two cuts (on edge) define the horizontal face of the steps.

4 The last two cuts define the depth of the steps. The cleaner these cuts are, the better. Otherwise some serious sanding will be necessary to make them look good under the black finish.

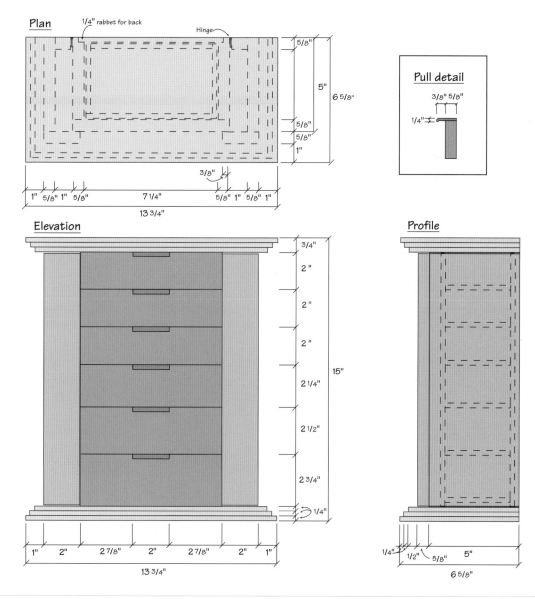

Plan

1/4" rabbet for back
Hinge

5/8"
5" 6 5/8"
5/8"
5/8"
1"

1" 5/8" 1" 5/8" 7 1/4" 5/8" 1" 5/8" 1"
3/8"
13 3/4"

Pull detail

3/8" 5/8"
1/4"

Elevation

3/4"
2"
2"
2"
2 1/4"
2 1/2"
2 3/4"
1/4"
15"

1" 2" 2 7/8" 2" 2 7/8" 2" 1"
13 3/4"

Profile

6 5/8"

1/4" 1/2" 5/8" 5"
6 5/8"

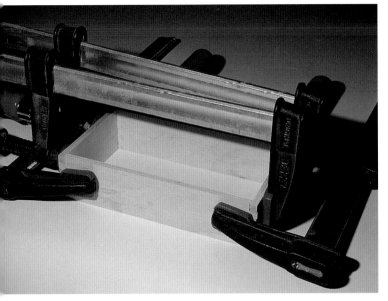

5 The construction of the drawers is the next step. After cutting the finger joints, glue and clamp the drawer sides, fronts and backs. Again, sand the interior faces of the drawers before you start gluing.

6 With all the drawer boxes assembled, tack the bottoms in place. Make sure the boxes are equally spaced to square and define the tongues of the drawer bottom guides.

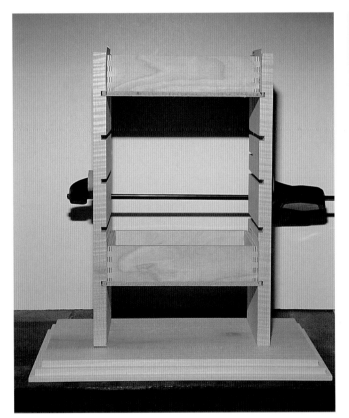

7 Once assembled, the drawers determine proper spacing of the interior sides in relation to the top and bottom. After determining the drawer spacing, drill clearance holes in the bottom and screw it to the sides (pilot drill into the sides). Use dowels and glue to attach the top from its underside only to hide the joinery, leaving a flawless top.

8 Before attaching the drawer fronts, use shims to equally space them. Work down from the top drawer. Drill clearance holes in the drawer box fronts, and use double-sided tape to temporarily secure the front while screwing the fronts to the drawer boxes. Remove the cabinet back to make it easier to push the drawers out without changing the front's spacing before finally securing it.

9 Finishing touches include lining the bottoms of the drawers with felt to protect the jewelry. Use small hooks attached to the inside of the doors to hang necklaces and bracelets. Felt pads attached to the underside of the bottom protect the surface of the dresser.

Armoire Assembly

Begin assembling the armoire by locating the sides on the top and bottom (photo 7). Use the back to square up the case, but don't nail the back in yet. Attach the top with dowels and glue.

You'll find a tight fit when screwing on the fronts. To solve this, mark a pilot hole while the front is "stuck" to the drawer box, then remove and pilot drill the fronts. An L-shaped screwdriver, ratchet screwdriver or long-shanked screwdriver held at an angle will ease this step. Next, drill and insert a small magnetic catch at the top of each door prior to hanging. Remember to pilot drill for all the brass screws, or you'll end up with a bunch of twisted-off screw heads. Once the doors are hung, locate the proper spot for the catch plate on the cabinet side.

cutting list (inches): *jewelry armoire*

No.	Item	Dimensions T W L	Material
2	Top & bottom	$^{3}/_{4}$" x $6^{5}/_{8}$" x $13^{3}/_{4}$"	Poplar
2	Interior sides	$^{5}/_{8}$" x $4^{3}/_{8}$" x $13^{1}/_{2}$"	Maple
2	Door sides	$^{5}/_{8}$" x 5" x $13^{3}/_{8}$"	Maple
2	Door fronts	$^{5}/_{8}$" x 2" x $13^{3}/_{8}$"	Maple
2	Door backs (hinged)	$^{5}/_{8}$" x 1" x $12^{1}/_{8}$"	Maple
4	Door tops & bottoms	$^{5}/_{8}$" x 1" x 5"	Maple
3	Drawer fronts	$^{5}/_{8}$" x 2" x $8^{1}/_{2}$"	Maple
1	Drawer front	$^{5}/_{8}$" x $2^{1}/_{4}$" x $8^{1}/_{2}$"	Maple
1	Drawer front	$^{5}/_{8}$" x $2^{1}/_{2}$" x $8^{1}/_{2}$"	Maple
1	Drawer front	$^{5}/_{8}$" x $2^{5}/_{8}$" x $8^{1}/_{2}$"	Maple
6	Drawer box sides	$^{1}/_{4}$" x $1^{5}/_{8}$" x 4"	Plywood
6	Drawer box fronts/backs	$^{1}/_{4}$" x $1^{5}/_{8}$" x $7^{3}/_{16}$"	Plywood
2	Drawer box sides	$^{1}/_{4}$" x $1^{7}/_{8}$" x 4"	Plywood
2	Drawer box front/back	$^{1}/_{4}$" x $1^{7}/_{8}$" x $7^{3}/_{16}$"	Plywood
2	Drawer box sides	$^{1}/_{4}$" x $2^{1}/_{8}$" x 4"	Plywood
2	Drawer box front/back	$^{1}/_{4}$" x $2^{1}/_{8}$" x $7^{3}/_{16}$"	Plywood
2	Drawer box sides	$^{1}/_{4}$" x $2^{3}/_{8}$" x 4"	Plywood
2	Drawer box front/back	$^{1}/_{4}$" x $2^{3}/_{8}$" x $7^{3}/_{16}$"	Plywood
5	Drawer bottoms	$^{1}/_{4}$" x 4" x $7^{5}/_{8}$"	Plywood
1	Drawer bottom	$^{1}/_{4}$" x 4" x $7^{1}/_{4}$"	Plywood
1	Armoire back	$^{1}/_{4}$" x $7^{7}/_{8}$" x $13^{1}/_{2}$"	Plywood
6	Handles	$^{1}/_{4}$" x 1" x 2"	Poplar

cutting list (millimeters): *jewelry armoire*

No.	Item	Dimensions T W L	Material
2	Top & bottom	19 x 168 x 349	Poplar
2	Interior sides	16 x 112 x 343	Maple
2	Door sides	16 x 127 x 340	Maple
2	Door fronts	16 x 51 x 340	Maple
2	Door backs (hinged)	16 x 25 x 308	Maple
4	Door tops & bottoms	16 x 25 x 127	Maple
3	Drawer fronts	16 x 51 x 216	Maple
1	Drawer front	16 x 57 x 216	Maple
1	Drawer front	16 x 64 x 216	Maple
1	Drawer front	16 x 67 x 216	Maple
6	Drawer box sides	6 x 41 x 102	Plywood
6	Drawer box fronts/backs	6 x 41 x 183	Plywood
2	Drawer box sides	6 x 47 x 102	Plywood
2	Drawer box front/back	6 x 47 x 183	Plywood
2	Drawer box sides	6 x 54 x 102	Plywood
2	Drawer box front/back	6 x 54 x 183	Plywood
2	Drawer box sides	6 x 61 x 102	Plywood
2	Drawer box front/back	6 x 61 x 183	Plywood
5	Drawer bottoms	6 x 102 x 194	Plywood
1	Drawer bottom	6 x 102 x 184	Plywood
1	Armoire back	6 x 200 x 343	Plywood
6	Handles	6 x 25 x 51	Poplar

Finishing Touches

To make the armoire jewelry-friendly, add felt as shown in photo 9. After that, it's up to the box's new owner to arrange all her jewelry — just watch that you aren't talked into buying more. ■

modern storage
Tower

Much like a skyscraper, this tower manages to pack tons of office stuff into a tiny footprint.

THE LAST THING I WANT TO DO WHEN STARTING work at my computer is to clear out a place to work. Unfortunately, some years ago my piles of stuff overpowered what little storage space I had.

Enter this modern storage tower. It will tame almost any wild pile of junk, and yet it takes up less than 2 square feet of floor space. The open shelves are designed to hold magazine storage boxes you can buy at an office supply store. The CD drawer holds 38 CDs — that will handle an average collection of computer CD-ROMs. The see-through doors let you display stuff or protect a few books.

I built this project using the Little Shop That Could Mark II, a rolling workshop on wheels that contains only $1,000 in tools. It was featured in the September 1999 issue of *Popular Woodworking*. You can see the plans for this rolling shop on our Web site (www.popularwoodworking.com) or you can pick up a copy of the new book *25 Essential Projects for Your Workshop* (Popular Woodworking Books) that features complete plans for the Little Shop.

This tower project is great for the beginner because it gives you a chance to try out some simple techniques you won't learn anywhere else.

Get It Down to Size

First cut out your parts according to the cutting list. If you can rip and crosscut the plywood on your table saw, great (the Little Shop excels at this). Or you also could use a circular saw or jigsaw to get the pieces down to manageable sizes; then finish them up on the table saw. Either way, cut your pieces a little bigger than the given sizes so you can then trim off the rough factory edges.

Cut rabbets in the side, bottom and top pieces that will hold the back as shown in the photo. Then cut rabbets in the sides to hold the bottom in place (the top is attached later). Lay out the biscuit joint locations for the fixed shelves. First clamp the two sides and partition pieces together side-by-side; be sure the top and bottom are perfectly aligned. Use a piece of plywood as a fence (see photo 3) to hold the biscuit joiner in place as you make your cuts. I used three No. 20 biscuits at each location where a shelf met a side piece. Because the partition is biscuited on two sides, you'll have to flip it over after cutting biscuit slots on one side.

After the biscuit slots are cut, dry-assemble the case to find any problems that might occur during assembly. Make sure the bottom sits squarely in its rabbets and check the top to ensure it touches the two sides and partition evenly.

If everything is OK, glue and clamp the case together. Clamp up the case with it face down on your work surface. This en-sures the partitions and sides are all flush at the front. Check the case to see if it's square by measuring it from corner to corner.

Mitered Door Frames

While the glue is drying, cut out the parts for the doors. Miter $3/4" \times 1"$ strips of wood that have a $1/4" \times 1/2"$ rabbet cut on the back edge for glass or Plexiglas.

If you don't have a miter sled to cut the rails and stiles for the doors, screw a sacrificial fence to your miter gauge. Clamp stops to the fence for the different length parts. After the door parts are cut to size, it's time to cut the slots for the splines that will reinforce the joints. First cut some spline stock from some scrap maple that's as thick as the kerf made by your table

cutting list (inches): *modern storage tower*

No.	Item	Dimensions T W L	Material
2	Sides	$3/4"$ x $13^{1}/4"$ x 55"	Plywood
1	Bottom	$3/4"$ x $13^{1}/4"$ x $15^{3}/4"$	Plywood
1	Partition	$3/4"$ x 13" x $54^{1}/4"$	Plywood
6	Shelves	$3/4"$ x 13" x 7"	Plywood
1	Back	$1/4"$ x $15^{3}/4"$ x $55^{1}/4"$	Plywood
1	Top	$3/4"$ x $13^{1}/4"$ x $16^{1}/4"$	Plywood
1	Top front edge	$3/4"$ x $1^{1}/2"$ x $19^{1}/4"$	Maple
2	Top side edges	$3/4"$ x $1^{1}/2"$ x 14 $3/4"$	Maple
8	Feet	$3/4"$ x $2^{1}/2"$ x 4"	Maple
8	Feet brackets	$3/4"$ x $1^{3}/4"$ x $1^{3}/4"$	Maple
4	Door stiles	$3/4"$ x 1" x 13"	Maple
4	Door rails	$3/4"$ x 1" x 7"	Maple
1	Drawer front*	$3/4"$ x $6^{7}/8"$ x $12^{7}/8"$	Plywood
1	Box side	$1/4"$ x 12" x $1^{3}/4"$	Plywood
2	Box top & bottom	$1/4"$ x $6^{1}/2"$ x $11^{3}/4"$	Plywood
2	Box back & divider	$1/2"$ x 6 $1/4"$ x 12"	Plywood

*Cutting size before applying edging. Some fitting is necessary.

cutting list (millimeters): *modern storage tower*

No.	Item	Dimensions T W L	Material
2	Sides	19 x 336 x 1397	Plywood
1	Bottom	19 x 6 x 400	Plywood
1	Partition	19 x 330 x 1378	Plywood
6	Shelves	19 x 330 x 178	Plywood
1	Back	6 x 400 x 1403	Plywood
1	Top	19 x 336 x 412	Plywood
1	Top front edge	19 x 38 x 489	Maple
2	Top side edges	19 x 38 x 375	Maple
8	Feet	19 x 64 x 102	Maple
8	Feet brackets	19 x 45 x 45	Maple
4	Door stiles	19 x 25 x 330	Maple
4	Door rails	19 x 25 x 178	Maple
1	Drawer front*	19 x 174 x 327	Plywood
1	Box side	6 x 305 x 45	Plywood
2	Box top & bottom	6 x 165 x 298	Plywood
2	Box back & divider	13 x 158 x 305	Plywood

*Cutting size before applying edging. Some fitting is necessary.

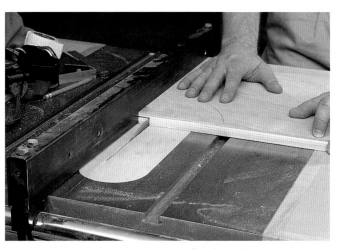

1 The Little Shop Mark II is a great system for cutting up large panels. Simply crosscut the 4x8 sheet to a little over the finished length and then rip the panels from the shorter piece.

2 After cutting the panels to length, cut $1/4"$ x $1/2"$ rabbets in the back edges of the sides, top and bottom to hold the back piece. Finish the rabbeting by cutting a $1/2"$ x $3/4"$ rabbet in the bottom ends of the sides for the bottom. When cutting rabbets this way, watch out for the falloff flying back at you.

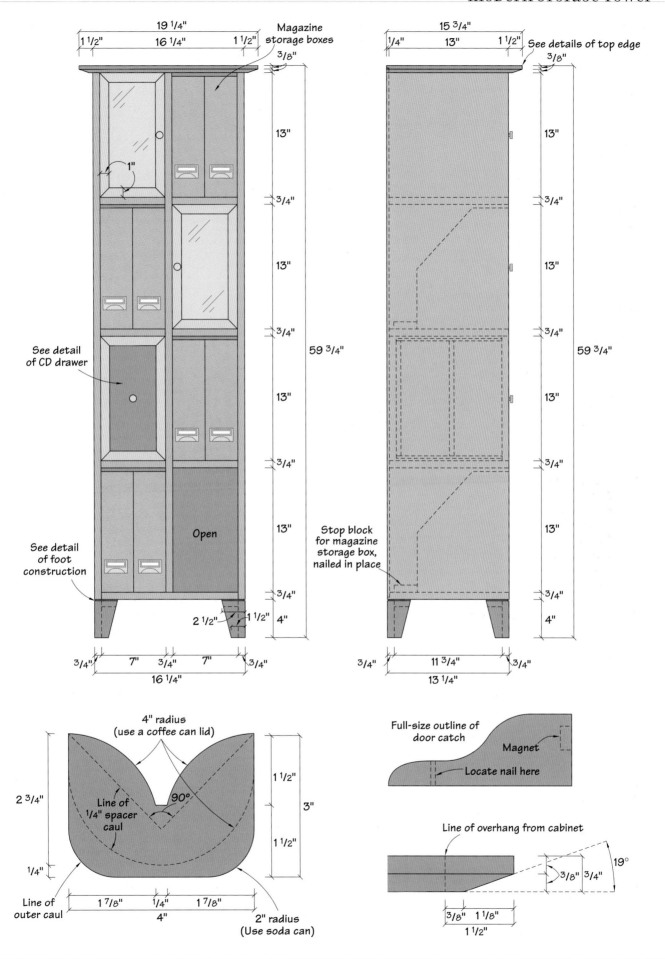

19 1/4"
1 1/2" 16 1/4" 1 1/2"
Magazine storage boxes
3/8"
13"
3/4"
13"
3/4"
1"
See detail of CD drawer
13"
3/4"
Open
See detail of foot construction
13"
3/4"
2 1/2" 1 1/2" 4"
3/4" 7" 3/4" 7" 3/4"
16 1/4"
59 3/4"

15 3/4"
1/4" 13" 1 1/2"
See details of top edge
3/8"
13"
3/4"
13"
3/4"
Stop block for magazine storage box, nailed in place
13"
3/4"
13"
3/4"
4"
3/4" 11 3/4" 3/4"
13 1/4"
59 3/4"

4" radius (use a coffee can lid)
2 3/4"
Line of 1/4" spacer caul
90°
1 1/2"
3"
1 1/2"
1/4"
Line of outer caul
1 7/8" 1/4" 1 7/8"
4"
2" radius (Use soda can)

Full-size outline of door catch
Magnet
Locate nail here

Line of overhang from cabinet
19°
3/8" 3/4"
3/8" 1 1/8"
1 1/2"

121

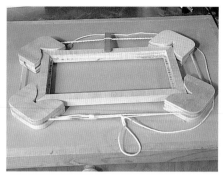

3 Clamp a straightedge to the marked line indicating the bottom of the shelf. Place the joiner up against the straightedge to make the cut. Cut slots in the shelves by placing them on a flat surface and repeating the process, indexing the joiner and shelf on the same surface.

4 Use a two-piece jig shown above. Hold the door parts at 45° and gently push them through the saw blade, leaving a saw cut 1/2" deep.

5 When you have a door glued together, place cauls on each corner. The groove in the back will evenly distribute the pressure from the rope on the joint. The curved indexing surface ensures that the clamp always provides pressure at the same point on the joint.

6 Place the doors back-side up onto a flat surface. Lay a small bead of clear silicone into the rabbet. The stuff I use comes out white, but dries clear. Cut the pieces to size and lay them into the rabbet on the back side of the door. Place a small piece of plywood on the Plexiglas to protect it, and place a weight on the plywood to apply pressure while it sets. When the caulk is dry, apply a bead to the other side of the Plexiglas, sealing it into the door.

7 To apply the veneer, simply lay down a bead of woodworking glue. Spread it out with a brush or a handy finger. Lay the veneer on the edge and apply high heat (not the baseball kind) to the edge with a common clothes iron. When you see the glue start to bubble out of the joint, the veneer is almost set. Leave it on a little longer, and apply pressure with a roller or a screwdriver shaft will work in a pinch.

Hanging a door using loose pin hinges

1. **Lay out and cut the mortises for the hinges.**
2. **Separate the top hinge and attach half to the case mortise and half to the door.**
3. **Hang the door by the top hinge and use this location to index the bottom hinge placement.**
4. **Screw the bottom hinge in place and you're done. This method makes sure the hinges won't bind while hanging the door.**

saw's blade. It helps to cut it a little thick and sand or plane it to thickness. Remember to have the spline's long grain run across the joint in the door. This provides the strongest joint possible. Cut the slots for the splines using your table saw as shown in photo 4.

Now glue the doors together. To do this in one step you need to make small tulip-shaped clamping cauls as shown in the diagram on page 121. These cauls push the miters together no matter where the clamping pressure comes from. The other neat thing about these cauls is that you use a length of rope to provide the pressure. Simply twist a small stick into the rope like

you would on a bow saw, and turn it until you get as much or as little pressure as you want. After the glue is dry, remove the clamps and clean up the doors with a chisel and plane.

Covering the Edges
When you're done with the doors, go ahead and add some solid wood edging to the top piece. Cut the 3/4" × 1 1/2" edging for the top, miter the edging and attach it to the top piece with biscuits. Now cut the chamfer on the front and sides as shown in the diagram on page 121.

Now do the edging. Cut the edging from 1 3/16"-thick stock in 1/32"-thick strips.

Rip this edging from a wider piece of wood. To be on the safe side, rip the edging on the outside edge of the blade — don't set your fence for $1/32$" and cut it that way. You apply this edging the same way you apply commercial iron-on edging: using adhesive and heat. The only difference is you supply the yellow glue and the edging as shown in photo 7. Glue the long edges to the case first. Clean them up with a chisel and file. Cut the edging for the shelves and apply them next.

Details

Screw the top in place, plug the holes and cut the plugs flush. Now fit the doors in their openings. The object is to have a $1/16$" gap all the way around. Hang the doors using loose pin hinges (these will make the doors easier to install). One problem these hinges cause with a small gap is that one edge can bind against the partition. You can remedy this by planing or sanding a little radius on that inside edge to allow the door to swing freely. Install the pulls, and make a couple of shop-made stops with rare-earth magnets. Nail and glue the stops behind the screw heads on the door pulls and use them to hold the door closed.

Make the feet from a glued-up L-shaped piece of solid wood. Rip a 45° bevel on two pieces of $3/4$" × $2^{1}\!/_2$" × 25" maple. Biscuit them together and glue them up using the rope and cauls you used on the doors. It's possible to use one long piece of rope to do the entire glue-up. Just keep knotting the rope strategically and rewrapping it around the next caul. Cut the feet to length, and cut a $1/8$" × $1/8$" rabbet in the top outside edge of each foot. Cut the tapered profile shown in the diagram. Glue and nail a corner block to the inside corner of each foot. This block allows you to screw the foot to the bottom of the case. Glue and screw the foot flush to the case corners.

CD Drawer and Finish

Now make the CD storage drawer; this is a small plywood box that accommodates plastic CD racks screwed into the box sides. You will have to cut these plastic rails down one space to fit the design of the tower.

Make the drawer front first. Simply take the front piece and cut a 1" × $1/32$" rabbet on the front of the door. Apply veneer to the small rabbet, simulating the

outline of a door with a solid panel, and apply iron-on edging to the top and side edges. The front requires stopped grooves be routed in its back side. Do this using a router in a router table. Build the box according to the diagram and hang it in the case using $1/2$" drawer slides on only one side of the box. This opens up the other side for the CD racks. Screw them in place and make sure a CD fits OK.

Sand the entire unit. Apply three coats of clear finish. It's easier to finish the back separately and install it when you're done.

When the finishing is done, glaze the doors using silicone. For this project, it was just as easy to use Plexiglas. Rehang the doors when the silicone is dry, and you're ready to clear off that computer desk to get the day's work done. ∎

supplies

Lee Valley (800) 871-8158

- 3 - Drawer pulls 01W13.01, $1.10/each
- 1set - 12" drawer slides 12K36.12, $10.25/set
- 2 pairs - CD rails 00S50.01, $3.95/pair.

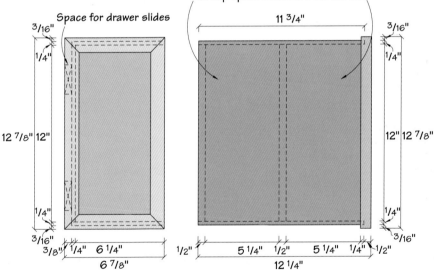

shoji-paper
Lamp

Light up your life (or a room) with this simple yet elegant lamp.

BELIEVE IT OR NOT, THE idea for this lamp came to me while scrutinizing some flea-market lampshades made from used Popsicle sticks. The concept, I decided, was sound. But I wanted to make some changes.

So instead of gorging myself on 100 Dreamsicles, I decided to use ¼" maple strips. And instead of creating a true oddity of Americana, I chose to look to the Far East to create a lamp that would be at home in a Japanese household.

Cut the Sticks

First you need to cut the 88 sticks that make up the sides. Rip some $\frac{1}{4}$"-thick maple into $\frac{1}{4}$"-wide strips. I found that a board that's $\frac{1}{4}$" thick, 6" wide and 4' long makes one lamp. Now crosscut the strips to $6\frac{1}{8}$" long.

Drill Holes for the Dowels

Now drill the 176 holes in the side pieces for the four dowels that hold the lamp together. I made a jig to hold a side piece in place on my drill press while I drilled the holes. The center of each $\frac{1}{8}$" hole is located $\frac{3}{16}$" in from each end. Now sand all the pieces.

Build the Base

First cut the base to size, and cut two $\frac{1}{4}$"-deep by $\frac{3}{4}$"-wide grooves in the bottom of the base. These should be located $\frac{7}{8}$" from the edges. Glue the feet in place. Now mark on the base where the four dowels will be located. Here's how: Draw two lines between the opposite corners of the base. This creates an X at the center of the board. Measure out $4\frac{1}{16}$" from the center on each of these four lines. Drill a $\frac{1}{8}$" hole at each location.

Sand the Dowels

Sand your four $\frac{1}{8}$" dowels a bit and put some wax on them. Slide the side pieces onto the dowels. When you've reached your final height, glue the four dowels into the base. Glue the top two side pieces to the dowels and cut them flush to the top.

Attach the Paper

Glue the shoji paper to the inside of the lamp. I cut out four pieces of paper and glued them to the inside using yellow glue sparingly. Add your light fixture and you're done. No finish is required. ∎

supplies

Highland Hardware, (800) 241-6748
- Shoji paper, item #21.64.01, $11.95 for a $11\frac{1}{8}$" x 60' (282mm x 18.3m) roll
- Light fixture available from Lowe's or other home warehouses. I used an Angelo brand 6' (1830mm) cord set with candelabra base, item #70108, $3.98.

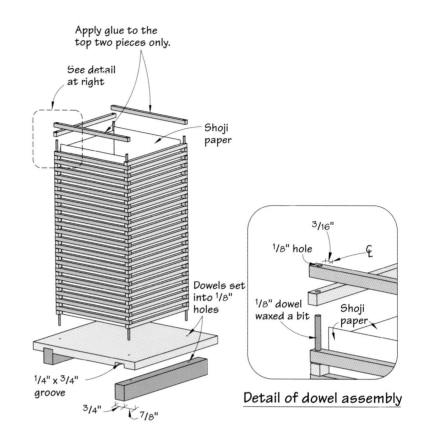

Apply glue to the top two pieces only.

See detail at right

Shoji paper

Dowels set into $\frac{1}{8}$" holes

$\frac{1}{4}$" x $\frac{3}{4}$" groove

$\frac{3}{4}$" $\frac{7}{8}$"

$\frac{3}{16}$"

$\frac{1}{8}$" hole

$\frac{1}{8}$" dowel waxed a bit

Shoji paper

Detail of dowel assembly

cutting list **(inches):** *shoji-paper lamp*

No.	Item	Dimensions T W L	Material
88	Sides	$\frac{1}{4}$" x $\frac{1}{4}$" x $6\frac{1}{8}$"	Maple
2	Feet	$\frac{3}{4}$" x 1" x $8\frac{1}{2}$"	Maple
1	Base	$\frac{1}{2}$" x $8\frac{1}{2}$" x $8\frac{1}{2}$"	Maple
4	Dowels	$\frac{1}{8}$" x 13"	

cutting list **(millimeters):** *shoji-paper lamp*

No.	Item	Dimensions T W L	Material
88	Sides	6 x 6 x 155	Maple
2	Feet	19 x 25 x 470	Maple
1	Base	13 x 470 x 470	Maple
4	Dowels	3 x 330	

INDEX

More great furniture projects from
Popular Woodworking Books!

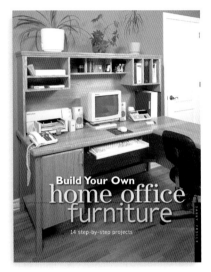

Transform any room into the perfect workspace! Inside you'll find invaluable tips and advice, plus 15 fresh, functional, fun-to-build projects packed with detailed photographs and step-by-step instructions. Designs range from simple storage modules to a computer desk/workstation, so no matter what your level of skill, you'll find plenty of woodshop excitement.

ISBN 1-55870-561-9, paperback, 128 pages, #70489-K

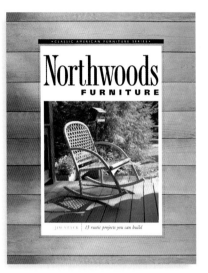

Northwoods furniture is functional and solidly built, embodying everything you value about life away from the fast-paced world. These 13 step-by-step projects can give you that kind of life with just a weekend in the woodshop. Each one uses basic woodshop tools, time-tested construction techniques and a variety of attractive woods.

ISBN 1-55870-569-4, paperback, 128 pages, #70500-K

Add charm to your home and new life to your woodshop with these exciting, attractive projects! Each one is faithful to the Country Furniture tradition, mixing classic lines with straightforward construction techniques. You'll find an incredible range of designs, some simple but clever, others exquisite and heirloom-worthy.

ISBN 1-55870-585 6, paperback, 128 pages, #70521-K

Turn your woodshop scrap lumber into simple, inexpensive pieces of furniture that are both sturdy and attractive. These 15 intriguing projects include a wide variety of tables, a bedspread valet, a desk, a mirror frame and more. Author and woodworker Arnold Sussman's project assembly methods are unique, using only a few saw cuts and glue.

ISBN 1-55870-543-0, paperback, 128 pages, #70404-K

These books and other Popular Woodworking titles are available from your local bookstore, online supplier or by calling 1-800-289-0963.